"IT'S ALL GOOD"

KEEPING THINGS SIMPLY REAL TO KEEP THEM REALLY SIMPLE

BY

VICKI POSTON

EDITED BY

JUDY R. ALVORD

PHOTOGRAPHY BY

JUDY R. ALVORD

GRAPHIC ARTIST

ELIJAH THOMPSON

DEDICATION

*In ever-loving memory of my sister, **Terry**, who is
and will always be with me. Your embracing love
carries me through each and every day of my life.*

THANK YOU

The path to "IT'S ALL GOOD" has been made all the more beautiful by the people who have been with me, step by step, all along the way. I could never feel proud of this project without recognizing those who have helped to make my dream become a reality. A very special and sincere thank you and dedication to one of the best friends anyone could ever ask to have, Jesus Christ, whose guidance was immeasurable.

Also a very special thank you to my incredibly talented friend Judy R. Alvord (Editor), who helped make this project happen. The amazing cover was also created with photography by Judy R. Alvord and Elijah Thompson (Graphic Artist). You both rock!

Endearing thank you's are extended to my parents, Ken and Chris Poston, my loving sister Karen and her husband David, and a special dedication to my cousin Robbie, (may God continue to rest your soul).

Warmest thank you's are also extended to other friends including but not limited to Tracy and Buddy M., Judy R. Alvord (Editor), Aunt Lucy and Uncle Zeke, Aunt Nora Lee, Aunt Net, Aunt Wilma, Aunt Roberta, cousins Tammy (and Duron), Ellen, Ann, Wayne, Cathleen K., Derek E., Jack and Leigh H., Julie and Rick S., Marcel J., Vicki (Bekiz) M., Nancy P., Sequoa P., Jeanie H., Merrylynn and Steve S., Wayne C., Mary F., Leisa and Ralph D., Sally O., Kim and Mike G., Cathy and Mike G., Lisa I., and Robert P. C. III., Linda and Tom B., Jason R., Biscuit and Baker, Sam and Barnaby R., Rea Rea, and Montana Pie.

TABLE OF CONTENTS

FORWARD

This book depicts my mere observations over many years of consulting and befriending the world around me. I have noticed that many businesses and individuals are not able to find simplicity in resolving the everyday issues at hand...not to mention trying to overcome the challenging obstacles we encounter every day. Keeping simplicity in mind, I recognize that if we will keep things real and simple, it ultimately results in goodness, confidence in our-self, and increases our faith in God. Keep it "real and simple; it's all good, through God". My purpose here is to hopefully share with you that finding out how to keep things simply real will ultimately teach you how to keep things really simple. This book is spiritual, motivational, inspirational and humorous. It has been one of the most challenging projects I've ever been inspired to achieve. I hope to spread spirit and enlightenment to others with realistic issues as well as my own personal views of them by adding a tangy twist of humor, a tingly ray of warmth, and ultimate integrity as we travel through this precious journey called "LIFE" that we've been so graciously given.

WARM BEGINNINGS

I began playing music at a very young age...the piano, guitar and trumpet, respectively. As a teen, I played my trumpet in many weddings including my sister's wedding. I wrote music and lyrics and had a copyright on them at the age of 16. I won many awards in high school including " Who's Who in Music Award", some district and state awards in stenography and word processing, was the senior drum major in the marching band and was the president of "Future Business Leaders of America".   With that said, I learned a great deal about leadership roles and overall communication skills. At the time it was merely fun and somewhat challenging, but was even more so later in my life's journey as my eyes began to widen and my periphery began to expand. Attending short classes in my senior year of high school was an exciting luxury because we were allowed to escape the academic atmosphere and work in the "real" world for the remainder of the day. T'was more fun than marching and sweating on the football field for hours during band practice or wishing the day away studying in a boring classroom. As drum major, having to stay physically fit was important, but it was so nice to work in a cool office rather than staying heavily armored in my uniform in the heat. It was however, great fun and it was all good. By the end of senior year I was quite tired of school and therefore decided to work full time for a while rather than immediately enter the college arena.

SWEET DREAMS

While in high school, I once went on a horseback riding adventure with a very dear friend; one whom I was getting ready to proudly graduate with. During this adventure I found myself reminiscing about the previous year when I tearfully saluted my graduating elders by playing the French horn during our Alma Mater. I knew their spirit and friendship would always be remembered and cherished. We had taken long, deserving beach trips together and enjoyed bouncing off of each others energy, humor and talents. We knew that we might never see or speak to each other again. And we also knew that no one could ever fill their gold-plated shoes. Their achievements, accomplishments and goal-driven aspirations were quite outstanding.

Without interpretation, this was clearly a very positive, spiritual and memorable learning process that would impact our lives in many ways and perhaps take us a long way in various aspects and elements in our lives. I remembered the absolute spirit and warmth I felt as I played the French horn for my cherished friends, extending my personal salutations with honor, with strength, with pride, and with heart-felt spirit while witnessing their inspirational being and yet our dreaded departure. I felt that perhaps in releasing their comforting hands which had always guided me and savoring their spirit that I knew would cushion my tomorrow; learning how they re-inspired the fundamentals of friendship through communication, trust, leadership, loyalty, and positivity, that they had once again instilled the spirited union of family. We challenged each other to complete the composition of any song, or poem, or just to be the best at what we can be in life and to follow our dreams and goals no matter what it takes to simply make things happen. Our mission is to make things happen and help others do the same. Helping others feel warm and spirited by simply keeping things real and simple is priceless. At least that's what Karma once told me.

The horse I was riding that day was so beautiful and majestic. I don't think God has ever created an ugly horse- feet and hair perhaps, but not horses. My friend and I gazed through the colorful , pine-scented forest with grace and anticipation of our futures, wherever our individual paths would take us. And we overlooked the fact that neither of us had much experience riding horses. Then all of a sudden my beautiful, majestic horse became ignorant and defiant as we approached a large fallen

10

tree which had left an obstacle literally shaped like the letter "H" neck-level to me. All I could anticipate was blood and mud, yet somehow I could hear laughter along the way.

Although I had guided him AROUND the tree and not UNDER it, he became aggressively defiant and graced his fat tail UNDER the tree, choking me backwards which tossed my tail into a reservoir of mud and who knows what else. So much for the white school shirt I was sporting! This was so not funny. I love horses but I was NOT liking this one. He continued to race through the woods and all I could do was chase my muddy, Tammy Faye self after him. He was my rented responsibility and I couldn't afford to buy a steak out of my parent's freezer, much less a horse. This was clearly upsetting, ridiculous, and demeaning! Exhausted by my seemingly 3-mile chase with Mr. Ed, we ended up at the stable where I learned that no one knew if the exhausted, defiant horse had eaten all day because he had been rented out all freaking day. I thought, "Seriously"? Where is my $75 for this oversight in all due respect? Subsequently, they briskly sprayed the mud and indignity off of me with a water hose as I collected my 20 bucks back and left. I had to cover my neck injury with makeup for my senior photo shoot. I wish I had known what I know now. Feed your livestock, please! In retrospect, I should have told them to keep the $20 and go buy some carrots and sugar cubes. It was ultimately hilarious and it was all good.

LIFE INSIDE INSURANCE

The effort and energy I had initially given to the working force slowly began to diminish, and I eventually realized that I was becoming exhausted. Subsequently, I obtained an insurance job from a well-known insurance company working out of a local agency. Soon after, I obtained my state property and casualty insurance license as requested by the agency owner and required by the state. The owner's name was Jack. He was an elderly, cantankerous man with a bad back. I eventually wrote a cute little jingle which he loved and we would sing in the office about his chair; a chair filled with water for his back, for which he had paid a fortune. We all rocked and worked well together and made him a large sum of money. In turn he treated us quite well. Jack immediately observed my sales talents and techniques which I had failed to realize myself and he always whispered sales tips to me in 3 words or less. He taught me boatloads of information in just a small amount of time. Although he was an old fart sometimes, I always felt like sliding him $75 as a mere consultation fee for his candid advice. He used to say "I may not always be right, but I'm never wrong." I don't know anyone else who thinks that way...or has that logic. No one at all. By this time life in insurance started to get really interesting and challenging.

Our insurance office was located in a large mall and was therefore open to the public. I literally witnessed people's false teeth fall into their laps while trying to pay their premiums, and of course I had to deal with heated upsets. There were times when I had to give tactful, yet embarrassing hints that "xyzpdq" meant please zip up your pants-we don't want to see your glory. One of the worst things about the job was pretending you didn't smell your client pass breathtaking gas as you were nearly stroking out, trying to think of a good reason to dash away from the fumes and make a quick copy of something for them. Handling heated conversations was never a problem for me however, trying to maintain my composure when clients came in so humbly just to get renter's insurance on their beloved television or typewriter- alone- was just difficult. Bless their heart; there was always a policy for their need. Learning to keep things real and simple and to keep it all good became my virtue.

There was a time when I was called to come into the office early during a major snow storm. Before the call, I had already begun to do a happy dance because we all just knew the entire city would be shutting down due to inclement weather, the monstrous snow storm. My boss, Jack, actually picked me up at my apartment and my excitement that the office would be closed due to the wintry, snowy mix just dwindled. We had to process a massive amount of auto claim reports and were swamped. We were the personal and initial source of contact for the disgruntled claimants who were expeditiously filing auto insurance claims during the brutal half-inch snow storm. They apparently did not understand that it is actually possible to drive here in the south with one inch or so of snow on the ground and that they should have respectfully taken precautions while driving. Simply said, if you're not used to it, pull up and peruse www.useyourjudgement.com. A northerner once told me that when southerners drive in the snow they are like instant idiots. Just add water. Keep it real, keep it simple and try to make it all good.

They also weren't aware that during, and as a result of snowy times in the south, the bread and milk stores make boatloads of profits, as do the handsome meteorologists who broadcast way too much (in some instances) unnecessary information, while elaborating their dramatic and energetic forecast. By the way, try muting your remote control and watch the excited meteorologists on the news some time during their broadcast of a snow storm. I did it by mistake one day and swore they were in a parade directing traffic! Whether it snows or not I think they get paid a commission for getting folks overly excited.Seriously, how much, if any snow will we get? Will we be able to make a snowball or have a "snow day"?

Come on...will it be 2 inches or one foot? No offense to anyone because I respect my meteorologists and by all means the beautiful south, but I get more comedic relief in watching them dramatically do a happy dance during their forecast than I do in watching cartoons.Just keep it real, keep it simple, and by all means keep the comedy rolling my way.

Now back to the snowy claims intake at the office. We were expeditiously working with customers and their overwhelming details as they flooded in with their auto claims, demanding immediate attention and thinking they were the only person in this world. And as always, it was the other person who was driving like the Clampetts' on The Beverly Hillbillies. Of course we embraced each claimant by giving them personal attention and absolute satisfaction so as to not make them FEEL like a "Clampett." Bless their hearts. There was no time for anything other than mere compassion and support.

One very important thing I began to learn was that things aren't always about YOU. It's important that we place ourselves in others shoes sometimes to understand circumstances without scrutiny. Additionally, we sometimes tend to make things our business when they don't even remotely involve us at all. The ("What about me"?) syndrome, you know. Things aren't always about us as individuals. And by the way, you can probably find that detail at www.getoveryourself.com. Keeping mindful and exercising that attitude will keep you well-spirited and emotionally flourished and gratified. Is it so hard for consumers to simply say "thank you" to our service rep's, tell them they're doing a great job and that you had a positive customer experience? For many folks, it seems to be easier to fault them for something quite petty and/or misconstrued than to applaud their confident and respected character. Simply send their boss a quick kudos (it's just a click or phone call away) indicating a positive customer experience rather than sending a note to the Oval Office telling their superiors that they were rude, just because they were bold and wouldn't tolerate your ignorance. I'm just saying...Over many years of folks in general, I can't believe how consumers can be so nasty. And remember, perception plays a huge role here as well. What one person perceives as ill-mannered or rude may seem entirely different to another set of eyes. Frankly, they must not know who Karma is! I have been on the kudos board before and it's a nice rewarding feeling; a very effortless and appreciated, warm applaud.

While taking claims I learned many meaningful and once again effortless ways to be a servant to others, not only in a professional manner but in a spiritual manner through being the Christian I was raised to be. God tells us to "do unto others" as you would have them "do unto you". An example is how to hold someone's hand selflessly and without effort, guiding them with spirit and compassion through confidence and leadership. Giving another person assurance that their tomorrow can be bright and happy is just practicing one simple logic--keep things real and keep it simple, knowing it's all good and for me, through God. Just giving someone a spirited air hug and an individualized smile, without expectancy, can make someone's day. Keeping it warm- spirited, simple, and all good.

While being inundated with claims, the late morning progressed. I quickly refreshed lipstick to my lips and hopefully not to my teeth. We were so busy with clients that we didn't recognize our hunger pangs. There was no time for even a Snickers Bar supplement or the apple that our doctor would have preferred us to have. I couldn't do any more than provide the level of service and dedication than what my multi-tasking Gemini-related energies encompassed me to do. While at the office I was dictating an auto insurance claim over the phone to our automated system and was required to announce the 17-digit vehicle ID number, enunciating all applicable letters as "D" as in David, "S" as in Sam...At the time I didn't realize how hungry I was and perhaps ignored the fact momentarily because I was busy being a servant and having fun doing my job. However, "S" wasn't for Sam and "D" wasn't for David. Oh my, what had I done?

While giving my 5 or so minute dictation, being professional and giving precise enunciation, my office companions became overwhelmed with laughter. The serial number I referenced had become an IHOP breakfast menu that I subconsciously created and my coworkers were crying with laughter. As my stomach growled all of the letters had become breakfast items . "S" as in sausage, "B" as in biscuit, "E" as in eggs and so forth. There were probably some grits and gravy on my menu as well. Hallelujah and pass the gravy, it was all good. I'll share a few more humorous stories that folks have found interesting over the years; some of which have been inspiring.

Within the insurance industry, I had been warned by my peers that working on the "Corporate" side would not be "as fun" as being on the agency side where I had spent the majority of my time. I wanted to get a feel of the corporate life so I traveled to Charlotte and interviewed for a corporate position with a major insurance firm. This firm was setting up a call center and wanted me to grow with them, which sounded amazing. And so with great excitement, I rolled the dice, took the job, and relocated.

I was #18 or so on the growing totem pole at the call center and there were over 400 employees when I left six years later. During this time, I took great pride in the growth of the center and ultimately played a crucial role in many aspects of it, showing agents how we operated, explaining how our inbound and outbound calls were being monitored, showing them around to different teams and components, and explaining our "State of the Art" call center. I was promoted to a commercial insurance underwriter and then spent 10 long, hard weeks in Connecticut , training for sales and underwriting. I stayed in a nice hotel, studied like crazy and played my guitar for my fellow students when we gathered to have some fun. The class itself was lengthy but fun. It was all good. During my stay I learned how to boil eggs in a coffee pot with someone from the Philippines (who comically asked as we passed via tour boat, "is the Statue of Liberty your grandmother"? which was actually kind of accurate). We went whale watching (I once yelled "three o'clock"!)when the whale was actually from the 9 o'clock position. We got some great panoramic pictures of that one. We went to NY and I bought a gold bracelet from the lapel of someone's coat from which they were selling jewelry. I knew not to get upset later when my wrist turned green during a site-seeing event. I had fun with my Yankee classmates. It was an inspirational journey which will always remain warm and educational in my thoughts. I even taught my Yankee friends to say "hey y'all"! and "how's your mom-n-em"? I had made lifelong friends and made awesome life-long memories.

At the call center, I had become very good friends with many folks during its growth. Many of them knew my family and how much we like to have fun and joke when we were not plowing through cumbersome days in the professional world. I'll never forget what my sister did to me when I turned "30". Knowing she lived 2 hours away, I did not anticipate an early morning birthday surprise from her. On this particular 30th year of celebrating life (yet turning 29 once again) I entered the call center and fueled up with coffee to spirit my anticipated whirlwind of yet another stressful day. Entering the extremely large maze at the center of the office, I noticed what might have been 500 pictures of my Clampett, 13 year old Peppermint Patty head plastered on everyone's cubicle. As I walked around, gazing at these so-called decorations, I knew who the mastermind was behind this embarrassment. Of course it was my sister, Karen. So, I immediately began plotting my revenge. Her joke was actually creative and hilarious and it charged everyone's day. My revenge, I decided, was to ultimately get her back on the following April Fool's Day.

I knew that Karen was in a fairly new and exciting relationship. I called the receptionist at her office, whom I had known for years, and asked if she would play along with me. I would jokingly send her my usual fake $75 fee for her participation. I asked her to call my Sis that April Fool's Day and tell her that she had just received a dozen roses, special delivery. I could not wait to hear from her! I knew she had a long walk to fetch her "air flowers" and had time to process things along the way. When she eventually called me, she had gotten halfway across the facility to pick up her invisible flowers and realized it was me getting back at her on that foolish day.

16

Peppermint Patty didn't stand a chance though because Karen's prank was far better than mine. I could see her spunky, excited self, sailing through the halls to claim her prized, beautiful bouquet, but to no avail. Literally. NO VEIL in her horizon that day. It was all in fun and well-spirited.

OUR FAVORITE DAUGHTERS

My other sister Terry used to sequester one of her colleagues to orchestrate her April Fool's jokes...once calling me, representing himself as the manager of my bank, and advising me that my account was seriously overdrawn. Whatever! We've had some awesome times and have always been there for each other. I've learned so much from my sisters over the years. We've spent every Christmas together at our parent's home regardless of how near or far we had to travel. I have observed every detail, taking direction from them in many ways. Most important was how to be happy, keeping things real, keeping things simple and knowing that through God it will all be good. They "had my back" in growing up and essentially educated me with encouragement and spirit in very challenging, yet humorous ways, sometimes singing "Send in the Clowns" as they artistically applied their makeup; mindful I'm sure that they were at all times trying to set good examples for their kid sister. They exemplified that things will indeed be "all good" while advising and educating me of the vast differences between the various levels of school.

We had always had a very joyful, musical and spirited Christmas every year at home with our folks; each of us daughters humorously pretending to be the absolute "favorite" daughter-reading aloud each of our Christmas cards given by our parents as each precluded the actual verse by stating "to our favorite daughter" as if that verbiage was really written in the card. Once I read my card aloud pretending that it said "to our ONLY daughter." I was like, I'll show you who the favorite is. There was lots of love and jovial senses of humor as our parents grinned in wonderment of whose house the stork was supposed to have delivered us to. Never a dull moment as the folks had us in stitches just as much as we did them; always in the spiritual presence of Christ. I always knew I was the "favorite" though.

My folks would always tell me that. Just like they told my sisters. It was always fun and spirited with the joy of Christmas, music, awesome food and fellowship, not to mention the appreciation and respect of it all, and each other. You could never chisel the warmth and spirit from the memorable and cherishing times we all spent together-keeping it real and simple, knowing that it's all good, through God. He is always the center of our home.

GIVE US STRENGTH

One day, after buying a home in my new city, a lady from an estate planning company called me to set up an appointment to have my North Carolina Will prepared. During the appointment, as we sat on my patio, I served her a crab dip appetizer because she was famished and exhausted from a medical procedure she had earlier that day. She was so poised and professional. I was glad I had something other than ketchup in my fridge to offer her. As professionals often do, she seemed to take a personal interest in me and became noticeably observant in how stressed I'd become over my years in the insurance industry. It appeared she was qualifying me as her protege'.

Over time, I became good friends with her and her husband which ultimately pivoted my career towards her estate planning business. I enjoyed spending spirited time with them, helping her with fancy dinner parties and sharing laughter while she trained me as an estate planning consultant. She had owned her business for many years and was very accomplished at it. She trained me and soon I was meeting with folks in the comfort of their homes; consulting with them, taking care of their estate planning needs, and making sure folks slept comfortably at night after making necessary and sometimes exhausting, complicated decisions. My schedule was somewhat flexible but quite exhausting at times. Having to be a "velvet hammer" as necessary was quite challenging, i.e., having to give folks warm "air hugs" while advising them the importance of having these important documents prepared. I enjoyed the new arena of being out from behind a desk to working mostly in the comfort of someone's home (especially at Christmas). Once again, I found that embracing the concept that we must keep things simply real to keep them really simple made a lot of sense...knowing that it's all good, through God. That seemed to be quite helpful with what my clients had to process as well.

One bright Saturday afternoon, right before I had to head out to a business appointment, I got a phone call from a gentleman stating that he was with the Charleston Fire Department where my eldest sister lived in West Virginia. Yeah, right, and "I'm Hillary Clinton!" I thought. I noticed the voice on the other end sounded a lot like one of my sister's friends whom she would occasionally entice to reel me into one of her well-planned and well-disguised jokes. Just simply being spirited with laughter and humor, proclaiming she could always outwit my pranks...she would make you cry with laughter just hearing her laughter filtering in through the background of the actual prank itself. Her pranks were always fun and exciting.

As I slowly sat down on my sofa to merely engage in and inquire as to the nature of the phone call from the fireman, I suddenly found there was no humor whatsoever in this particular call. The proclaimed fireman on the other end advised me that there had been an apartment fire and that my sister was deceased.

He couldn't have been serious. No, in my mind's eye, he was not serious. "Who is this"? I asked as I bitterly snarled rising like a peacock, angrily engaging in this unrealistic conversation. As he continued to with little compassion, if I may say so, explain what had happened, he advised me that my phone number was the only one they found in her apartment which is why they were calling me. There had been an apartment fire, accidentally caused by her neighbor and my loving sister didn't make it out. Without a lot of unnecessary adieu, my bitter yet selfish thought was that "this only happens to OTHER families, NOT mine." Because my sister and I had joked quite often, I once again initially thought this was beyond a nasty joke yet boldly had to embrace this news with strength somehow...tons of it; the ton that God always embraces us with; the ton that we sometimes take for granted. It didn't seem real, it definitely wasn't simple and it wasn't at all good. How was I to tell my parents that they had lost a child? They had lost their first child, their prime, the center stone of us girls. And how was I to tell my beautiful, spirited sister Karen, that we had lost our BFF? Our eldest sister and confidant was supposed to live forever. How were we ever to cope through this hell? But God was there, somewhere, I knew. And I mean THERE- big and bold- for all of us. I had always told myself to never question God (as per the title of one of the songs I had written years ago) and to practice what I preach by keeping it simple, that it will always be good through God. And it's true. God was there and He will always make it good and simple if you keep your faith in Him.

Terry's neighbor, like I said, had accidentally caused a grease fire in his adjoined apartment. It was unfortunate that the odorless carbon monoxide didn't allow her to escape and sent her into a graceful, peaceful sleep from this Earth. Ms. Mother Nature herself, ultimately led Terry to awaken in peace and harmony in God's almighty, powerful arms, to be comforted upon cushiony pillows allowing her to sing triumphs and spirited praises in His marvelous Kingdom...tapping her foot to the joyous music as faithfully as she so spiritedly did here on Earth.

Although I felt my life soiled and ruined and my world shattered momentarily, it was simply keeping the faith and finding comfort in the goodness of life and treating each day as if it was my last; treating folks as if it was the last time I would see them or the last conversation I would have with them; and smelling that rose I never took time to smell. It only takes a quick second to smell the fragrant aroma of a simple rose. It felt however, like a very long lifetime, before I could smell that pleasant aroma again.

Terry and I looked tremendously alike according to what other folks thought and how we favored in some of our pictures. She was one of my best friends and one of the best people you would ever want to know. She was full of life, love, warmth, and spirit and so very gorgeous and smart. She was the first favorite daughter, always smiling and making things happen. She even headed some charities. She was about keeping things real and simple, knowing it's all good, through God. I sometimes get chuckled and can only imagine how entertaining she must be in the pillows of clouds in our beautiful Heaven and what she is making happen in her jovial, talented way.

My home would become inundated with friends anxiously awaiting her arrival when she would come to town. My friends would fill my house to be comforted and spirited by her love, compassion and her music. Terry was an accomplished pianist and an angelic, beautiful singer. She was in a high school play years ago with singer/songwriter Kathy Mattea. I happened to come across some pictures of Kathy and Terry on stage as I was channeling through some old photos. My sister's life was a blessing to everyone who had a chance to know her and feel her love, compassion, and friendship. She was blessed and was truly a blessing.

Two funerals were conducted in two different states because over the years she had acquired many friends and colleagues who lived in many states. She had a lot of respect from various charities to which she had selflessly dedicated so much of her time and passion. During the first funeral, held in the mountainous state of beautiful West Virginia, it became quite uncanny and somewhat exhausting to witness others staring at me as if they were looking at a ghost that somewhat resembled a deer in headlights. Needless to say there was no question that we were sisters. Many people

21

that I hadn't seen in many years attended this West Virginia funeral and I was introduced to many folks I had only heard about and many friends I hadn't seen in years.

The day after her second funeral, which was in South Carolina, I returned home and resumed preparing people's wills and trusts. How challenging that was. I would have rather been slapped than to sit across from folks and address those types of issues at that particular time, but it was what it was. Suffice it to say, it took me a while to personally practice what I'd always preached about smelling that rose... Again, it is what it is and we always have to be big people and remember those 5 little words, "it is what it is," period. Keep the faith, keeping it real and simple and exercising our patience, knowing that it will indeed all be good, through God. It may be hard, but it is imperative that we "let go and let God." Our faith is not an option. It is an absolute requirement.

PRECIOUS MOMENT

I was making a decent living as an estate planning consultant but as the economy declined, so did our salaries. People began drafting their own documents on computer software, many times not reading the fine print and later finding themselves in an unfortunate pickle. Subsequently, I was offered yet another estate planning job with a much larger local estate planning company. I was once again trained (in much more depth) and was the liaison for yet another firm of estate planning attorneys. I sold the estate planning documents, legal and tax services, and had a traveling radius of about 30 miles or so. My new company quickly recognized my compassion for the elderly and those who were underprivileged, therefore assigning me many appointments with those who were in the hospital or nursing home or under other medical assistance. My days began early and I sometimes didn't get home until after midnight. Whenever I went to some of the nursing homes it always felt so rewarding to simply tickle the ivory a few moments in hopes of seeing some warm smiles in a haven that probably never got a lot of personal attention.

I had one particular appointment at a gentleman's home that was extremely impressionable and very unforgettable. The details regarding this delicate and sensitive assignment, which my office had faxed to me that morning, indicated that the customer was a quadriplegic. It also indicated that some of his family members would be present during the appointment. Twas the first time I'd had the opportunity and privilege to assist someone in this extreme capacity. The living room in which he was bed-ridden and laid motionless encompassed several overhead monitors that displayed all outside activities in every angle of his home and each room inside. He couldn't move his limbs obviously, but he could move his eyes and kept himself occupied in viewing the activities. While drafting his paperwork and feeling the warmth of his home and the love and fellowship of his family members, he indicated his coherent replies to each of my questions with the meekness of his gestures. Gospel music pleasantly radiated throughout his home, setting such a soothing background tone. He began to sign his paperwork with a pen in his mouth and when finished, I gently removed it (giving him the dignity he deserved). Privately I conveyed that with my presence and other witnesses, all was good. I assured him that I appreciated the opportunity to have met him and his family and to have been of assistance in such a delicate situation. The admiration I felt for that family was absolutely tremendous.

Life was all good--flexible yet stable, structured and appreciated. I was on the board of directors at my neighborhood swimming pool. It was fun scheduling pool activities with the daycares and watching the children's swim teams. Not only did we have a Baptism for a local church, but we ran the concession stand, played with the kids, maintained chemicals in the pool and staffed the lifeguards. Merely getting to know folks in the neighborhood and acquiring a personal and professional rapport with them made life interesting, fun, and simple.

At the office, there were about 10 estate planning consultants. We had great comradery. We would feed off of each other's sales tactics during our weekly meetings and subsequently recorded an informative training CD for our customers on behalf of our company. Working "by the book" is how I was trained to do things. Knowing what was and was not marginal, making the right, accurate, ethical, oral and practical decisions was important. Using our fundamentals as learned in our teachings and guidance was essential. The office wanted me to learn to speak Spanish, like overnight, I felt. They called me and tried to send me on a Spanish-speaking appointment. "Seriously"? Give me $75 and I'll learn Spanish estate planning. Basically I had merely enough time to learn to ask "where is my suitcase"? That question alone wouldn't have gone over well in the home of a Spanish-speaking couple, I'm sure! As with all sales appointments, it is very crucial to know what is expected of you at each sales appointment, and if possible, try to have an idea of what the client's needs are. Inquire about their concerns, their history, and their desires. Keep it as simple as possible so as not to write a book about their individual situations. Know your product, have product knowledge, and have your resources readily available in case you don't have the answers to everything. Keep things real, simple, professional and flowing-and the keyword here is resources. Have them available or you will look like a Clampett-ass fool if you don't. One of the pertinent characteristics as a sales person is not only knowing and understanding your product, but establishing your level of confidence and boundaries, which will always keep you in your dignified comfort zone. Once again, having your ducks in a row, keeping your horse in front of the cart and knowing who and what your resources are is all a part of structure and well-being. How well you go by the book, (or know how to dance in the margin of having a little "wiggle room,") how well you are perceived by the customer, how well you know your product, delivery, and overall professionalism, how you deal with each and every question and/ or rebuttal and being a "velvet hammer" as needed will determine your success. Keep it real and simple knowing that it's all good.

Over time, I learned many important things that we sometimes take for granted, including things that can't be learned from a book or on the internet. Such things might include being open-minded, grounded, observant of people and their feedback (including body language), how truly long some people's noses are, how to avoid burning bridges, not to lose a phone number you may need tomorrow, and to be committed to your goals. Be organized. Be skilled, be prepared, and positive, positive, positive. Keep your glass half full and not empty. Simply look up a word that you may not know the meaning of. Don't be self-absorbed or judgmental, and look out for your neighbor, friend, colleague, and family member who has always had your back. Have their back too. Stop and smell a flower, open a door for someone and smile at an older person. Hug them even. It's really not hard. Be thankful that regardless of whatever life has dealt you, someone else may have it worse. Some may have it better, but it is what it is and the glass that you keep half full will positively quench your thirst.

What I am suggesting is that we genuinely exercise the fundamentals of life through spirit and faith, being generous, compassionate and sensitive, ultimately strengthening our aura, our identity, our pride, our livelihood, our reputation, our future, our happiness, our children's future, and that of our young entrepreneurs. We should always attempt to strengthen our life and help strengthen that of others. Many of us don't learn a lot of the important facts of life in a local coffee shop. When my friends and I exchange sentiments of these values, we simply charge the virtual $75 consultation fee, knowing that "the check" has always been in the mail.

These last several years have been quite challenging, to say the least. After eventually being chiseled down to jobless from a tenured totem pole of estate planning consultants, I was among the millions who had escalated into our unemployment ratio. Being physically centered and residing near an NFL football stadium and some of the nation's largest banking headquarters and businesses, I never imagined not having a job. With every interview I went to, there were 1000 others ready to do the same. Even for part-time jobs. I was mindful that I had been making a comfortable salary not very long ago and so were they. But, it was what it was.

I had an interview with a company advertising that the job was to sell "residential equipment." Of course they would never elaborate any details over the phone. Ultimately after wasting my time and energy, I found the job to be that of selling vacuum cleaners door to door or steak knives as an "Account Manager." Seriously, where's my check for the "bait and switch" ad? From selling fund-raising concert tickets for a fire department, to simply whatever it takes to keep Peter and Paul happy, I found out how exhausting during cumbersome times it can be to keep yourself prideful and dignified where the only desire is to be shielded from the judgment of others. Keep things real and simple knowing that through strength and determination, things will ultimately be good.

Communication is one of the most important keys to station in our everyday pocket of life. Stay focused with that fact because Karma will bite you in the tail someday if you don't-in my mind's eye, that is. Makes sense to me. Maintain your pride and dignity wherever you are in this world being mindful of your expectations and what is expected of you from your employer, your family, you relationships, your church, your friends and neighbors, and your schools and colleges. Think outside the box and be the best person you can be whether you're a sister, a daughter, a friend, a niece, a neighbor, a cousin, a mentor, or a colleague. Once again, know who and what your resources are. Keep God alive with the understanding that if He takes you "to it" He will take you "through it." As the saying goes, "let go and let God," always and forever. Play your part in life and trust that God had had your back and has ridden many waves with you..and always will.

A few years ago and shortly after I had unfortunately and unexpectedly been laid off of work due to the poor economy, I received a phone call from LB, one of my previous colleagues. LB had heard through the grapevine that I was doing some part-time telemarketing and appointment setting work. Knowing that I, like her, was a pro and velvet hammer at prospecting and selling, simply pulling the bull by the horns in a qualifying process and proficiently setting sales appointments, she contacted me and came to visit, fax machine in tow. What a dynamic duo. She was quite a true blessing and had been a great friend for many years. I was therefore happy to begin working with her immediately.

During this unexpected hurdle in life and keeping a humbled and positive outlook, I kept mindful that things always seem to work and pan out to the fullest, if only for a day. I was to keep striding into the opportunities of the future and keep afloat, staying positive, strong and dignified. "It is what it is" and all we can do is the best with what we have at any given moment and truly turn "it" into action with extraordinary commitment, devotion, and dedication. Sometimes it's hard to completely wrap your head around a given situation and hard not to have a negative attitude like "I didn't sign up for this." You can cry the river of Pity Canal all you want but again, it is what it is.

It's called the "circle of life" and reality is how the ball bounces. And once more, wherever you go, there your Clampett-ass is with you. Having a positive attitude will help you ride some large, powerful and perhaps cumbersome waves that just may end up carrying you to a powdery, white sandy shore. Again, being mindful not to burn bridges and remembering folks who have provided me with goodness and kindness and a refreshing glass of iced tea kept me focused so that I might leave them with a simple, yet warm hug and a genuine $75 smile in return. It's important to stay focused, open-minded, and grounded; being mindful, alert and humbled; embracing the fact that we are all essentially a union as a whole; working together and knowing there is never an "I" in team, no matter what circumstance. There is however, a "me" in "team", but let's not go there. What I had remembered from years past while working in corporate America and having to witness the rug being snatched from underneath my superiors is that the warm, generous hand you shook while climbing the corporate ladder may be the same cold hand you may unfortunately shake while trailing back down that wobbly ladder. Like I said, I was always thankful I was never a bridge burner and that my good friend Karma and I have always had a pleasant relationship. We are pretty tight. She's always been such a pleasant friend to have--not quite the proverbial "B" many folks have thought her to be. Perhaps she may be on up there with my other common-denominator friends as I highly regard and respect our closeness. Keep things real, and keep it simple. It's all good, through God.

THE SUN IS ALWAYS OUT

I treat every day with respect and rejoice and am glad in it, managing my time professionally and personally to the best of my ability. I knew that everything would come together again with time because this is God's playing field, not mine. I know that I am always ready for God to answer my prayers the way He plans- on His time clock and on His terms, not mine. That's never optional. I try to remain flexible, ready and open-minded for His cues and am always prepared to take His cue and direction and to take each individual skill and experience with me, in stride and with integrity and dignity. I carry that forward with me every day to help others know that it's about keeping things real and simple and in perspective. We can simply take a stumbling block and turn it into a stepping stone as we gradually and continuously learn from the experiences we encounter one step at a time. Know that life doesn't have to be a cold, circular rat wheel, but can often be a warm, exciting potter's guild or that warm, fuzzy puppy centered in your plate of life.

If you continue to do the same things in the same manner, you will continue to get the same results. Point blank. I could sugarcoat this, but it would only give you a cavity. Switch things up a notch and do something different in your pattern of life like simply hugging a Veteran you meet and thank them for their service. Say your prayers and be gracious and less judgmental. Focus on your own personal plate and not that of others. Regardless of what you are going through, there is always someone else who is going through something more crucial than your particular situation. We've all heard about the man who entered into a large room where many people were holding a bag of their own personal problems. After passing their bags around in hopes of swapping them out for someone else's, they were so happy to have regained their own bag at the end of the exchange. I often wonder how some people mentally endure the traumatic challenges in their personal lives like fighting a war, losing a limb, living through PTSD, or going from rags to riches and perhaps back to living out of a car again. But again, it is what it is, and if that's where we end up one day, well, at least we wake up breathing. Face reality the best way you can and try to learn something new every day. Stand toe to toe with your fears and embrace the challenge in the magnificent reflection of the stare.

Don't ponder and anticipate your life, or its' journey or destination. Live life and live it well, with compassion and to its' fullest. Treasure and nurture your values and turn them into action with extraordinary passion and commitment. Like the ole' cliche', "you have to spend money to make money." Sometimes we have to lose before we gain and we must take a couple of steps backwards to gain several steps forward. Remember that the sun (or SON) is always out but we just can't always see it. More importantly- live, love, and laugh knowing that it's better to have loved and lost than to have never loved at all.

Personally, I have not experienced some things of which I've written, but that of which I've witnessed. Some folks call it being street smart, not just book smart. The bottom line in my book is knowing that God is in my court and "THAT" indeed carries me a long way. We all have had challenging times and have experienced difficult situations. We've encountered, had to endure, and overcome. Knowing that God "will not" put more on our plate than we can handle helps us to become a stronger person and to find our purpose in life as we connect the dots of His given direction and guidelines. It helps us climb the tallest of mountains and to turn the other cheek (that we thought we'd run out of) to people of bitterness and judgment. It helps us to recognize the truth and goodness in all things. Have a sense of humor- laughter can be the best medicine. Being a consultant for many years, I thought that I had seen or heard it all until I'd hear another story. Stories told over and over again from many folks, many, many, folks. Sometimes unfortunate, demeaning, devastating, and traumatic situations happen. All we can do is pick ourselves up from any given situation, no matter how difficult it may be, and adamantly dust our bottoms off and put our foot forward into the next day; all the while asking and trusting God to help pick us up to continue with strength and glorification of His footprints. Sometimes we stay on "the beaten path" and feel like we're getting nowhere. Once again and in all simplicity, if we continue to do the same things in the same manner, what will we get? The same results. Patience is an absolute virtue. This we must always remember.

Not long ago, I reopened my home (which had also been my office/sanctuary) to a long-term, very dear BFF of nearly 20 years and offered my assistance as she had fallen from her mother's attic and broken her shoulder. It reminded me of the impact of the corporate fall in some ways. There is a fall; something gets broken; there is healing; and then there is moving forward. My dear friend, Tracy, had lived with me on and off for many years and has been like a sister to me, especially during and after the death of my beloved sister, Terry. Tracy had to undergo a very painful and extensive surgery after her fall to have rods placed in her shoulder. The extent of her pain was beyond chilling and petrifying to not only her, but to me as well. When someone is in such pain and there is nothing much that you can do, it hurts you too. She simply needed a place to stay with someone who could care for her and from what I found, someone who could monitor the administration of her medications.

After a few days of being on her medication, some of her dreams became not only verbal and somewhat animated but almost comical. When she started dreaming of flying turtles and returning phone messages in her sleep, and rolled onto the coffee table as if it was a gurney, I was glad to know that someone other than herself was taking good, competent care of her. I would sometimes turn the TV volume down so not to miss out on hearing her dreams--sometimes more comical than the sitcom that was playing. That's ugly, I know, but it was what it was and I so dislike to see people in pain.

Tracy and I have been best friends for many years and long-term friends of each others families. She had always been like a sister to Terry and me. That said, several years ago I had gone with Tracy to her mother's house for a visit. Her mother was in the first stages of dementia and it had been quite a long while since I'd seen her. She was so appreciative of my visit and welcomed me with warm hugs. She was so very alert and full of spirit, not what I expected. Often, she would softly stroke my hand as I smiled at her with warm air hugs in return. She looked vibrant and full of life, in spite of her condition. She would say nice pleasantries to me and it was just an overall wonderful, spirited, yet overdue visit. Her condition was almost unnoticeable at times. In fact, I had almost forgotten about her dementia. Those moments were so sweet and precious and she was so full of life and consciousness. We both felt the magnitude of such a blissful reunion and visit. Her old-time stories were very spirited and eloquently detailed. Quite frankly, it was nice to hear her kind voice and feel her spirited warmth at that particular time. After our very warm and overdue visit, Tracy and I took a refreshing stroll around the lovely neighborhood to get some fresh air. It was during our walk, to my dismay, that Tracy subtly reminded me of her mother's condition and advised me that her mother had been "out of her head" during our entire visit and didn't know who the heck I was--or remember me at all. Talk about bursting my joyous, yet naive bubble....quite a sad situation.

After many years of suffering, her mom eventually passed away. When Tracy called me early one morning, after returning from my long and exhausting trip to DC, I knew, as the phone rang, what had happened. She advised me of their mother's passing within the last hour and asked me to come over. In my solitude and in tearful remorse I looked up and exclaimed, "HALLELUAH" knowing that her Mom was now at peace and that she would once again smile and dance. I knew that she was now in a much better place; at peace and free from pain; and that she would get to hear my sister sing her angelic and welcoming praises. I was so proud of Tracy in that she had boldly gone to be with her frail, dying mother. With endless comforting embraces and hugs, Tracy was there to comfort her mother as she left her family and this earth. Tracy had prayed that her passing would be peaceful, and that her mother would be glorified in the sanctity of God's Kingdom. It was all good.

In weeks prior, Tracy would email me as she was notably crying that her mom was in so much pain. She knew my heart was crying on my side of town for them as well. It literally broke my heart and exhausted my energy on their behalf. That's a hard thing to endure, hugging your loved one as they cling to life, but God doesn't put anything on our plate that we can't handle. We both knew that my gold nugget of a sister would be there with bells on and Tracy and I were able to find peaceful comfort in that fact. God is great, isn't HE? And He will give you the guidance and wisdom if you have faith. When Tracy made that last minute phone call to me, I had already made myself clear to her, that aside from my busy schedule, I would always be there at the drop of a hat for her. Tracy had always been there for me, especially as my BFF, when Terry passed.

Years back, when Terry passed, I inherited a few of her belongings, one of which was a deep freezer. It was once white in color, but had turned jet-black due to soot after the fire of course. I remember the sickening aroma after it was brought to my home. The stench of it brutally reminded me of her devastating, traumatic death. Subsequently, I recall the subtle cries of Tracy as she scrubbed that freezer for many hours after my arrival from my late night estate planning consultation. Her $75 was so in the mail, a mere gesture for her introduction to hot bathes, loaded with Epsom salt which was quite the remedy for the tremendous muscle aches and for soothing the trauma of losing a loved one. Tracy spent roughly 6 hours that particular night sobbing endlessly, however the deep freezer was once again white in color. A friend in need is a friend indeed..and she is a BFF for all time. Treasure your friends and keep them forever. Let them know how special they are to you and remind them frequently. Cherish these gems and never let them go because awesome and true friends are so incredibly hard to come by these days. Never let them go and never take them for granted. No one is promised a life on earth forever. Speaking of gems, being the multi-tasking Gemini that I am, as are most other Gemini's, I always thought that whoever created pantyhose and Gemini's should be smacked. However, on a lighter and more positive note, I always tell folks that there is a gem-n-i, and there's a gem-in-you too. Although we all try to be a real BFF (and not a "Broke Friend Forever") we should simply try to do unto others as we would want them to do unto us. It's as simple as how we were brought up, (those of us who may be a little long in the tooth perhaps) being mindful and exercising the fundamentals of establishing and maintaining our friendships and our business pursuits. Learning comes not only from fundamental teachings but also by example itself--from our elders. That's how I was raised and how I operate and roll. That simple formula has personally worked for me, so far. Keep things real, and simple and it will ultimately all be good....especially if you have faith in yourself and faith in God. My incredible BFF sister Karen, my parents, including my God-parents, Aunt Lucy and Uncle Zeke were all instrumental (as was I) in having faith and comforting each other during our beloved Terry's tragic death.

Let your peeps know how truly dear they are to you and that they are indeed the best friends anyone could every have. I have several best friends and it is so important to know how to keep them and cherish their friendships. Let them know how much they are needed, respected and appreciated. Most people do not acquire lengthy and nurturing friendships or maintain a lengthy and nurturing marriage by keeping a clean car or a manicured lawn. Not that I know of any way! Live through and by the examples that were demonstrated by the fundamental teachings of our parents and elders that were instilled in us as youngsters, which they learned through the powerful Word of God. Cherish your relationships. Honor and respect them. Nurture them in an unselfish manner whether it is personal, professional and/or spiritual. Life comes and goes like the blink of an eye.

My parents instilled the importance of friendship in us as children. My parents were friends to each other and friends to us girls as well. They have been married for over 55 years and I'll give you $75 if you can count on one hand how many couples you know who have that longevity these days. I am so proud of their faithfulness to each other and happy that they are still here living a healthy life. They have been rejoicing in spiritual friendships with their best friends, Aunt Lucy and Uncle Zeke for over 50 years and with each other through their faith in the Lord. They still hold hands on the beach, a clasp of trust and warmth, honoring and respecting each other with love. Loyalty and communication are the major factors in their successful marriage and relationship. Although life is not always a pleasant boat ride, we can certainly find understanding and goodness by ascertaining that our glass stays half full and not empty. And by all means, just keep it full of something, whatever it is that you positively enjoy. Take time out for yourself and take a short vacation from work, especially if you find yourself entering your employee I.D. number on your microwave as you try to heat up a cup of coffee in the morning. I'm not saying that I've ever done that, however, I do have three days off coming up that I recently requested. I'm just saying.....

Once again, we all know that good friends are hard to find. A friend in need is a friend indeed. It's as simple as that. Although I have had to weed out a few friends, or acquaintances I should say, as we all do, I have noticed that I have an inadvertent qualifying process when establishing my friendships. They all have the same "common denominator." They're funny and they're overall smart. I didn't say they are " brilliant and hilarious." Just fun and level-headed. As we grow in life I can see where this type of observation can help us determine the types of people we grow close to and perhaps befriend them and to also steer away from those who might pose turmoil or drama to our lives. Again, it's the same type of qualifying process we sometimes use with our clients or customer. Our friends and our families are our angels on this Earth. Keep everything truly real, simply knowing it will indeed always be good through God.

Not long ago I had a lot of different types of big-girl things thrown at me at once. I had already sold my aged car to flip it for another car, but had to use that money to buy a new hot water heater for my house instead. This was just another financial burden that we all get faced with and have to struggle through. It's a hassle and worry, having to pay the proverbial "Peter to pay Paul" and to simply try to FIND which Peter to pay Paul with. Speaking of whom, I'd like to have a private prayer meeting with them someday. They can certainly work my Clampett- nerves when they catch me off guard.

Lots of financial things that we all have to struggle through were screaming at me, but it was what it was. Again, trying to find which Peter to rob for Paul, and sometimes simply "finding" a Peter to "pay" Paul can be downright exhausting. But, if you've pulled through tough times before, you'll pull through yet another troubling adventure, especially if you keep a tight hold on that glass half full of water. I mean wine. No, I mean water. No, no, whatever it is you're drinking, just keep your glass half full and not empty.

Be mindful that hard times are not only for today and that patience along with prayer is indeed a virtue. Even opening my home to tenants was sometimes like having five screaming kids in my house. I love children, for a while. Just as long as I can hand them back. During hard times it's important to not only keep spirited faith, but keep your lines of communication open and with an open mind, good things will eventually happen. Being a consultant for many years and dealing with tons of folks on a weekly basis, I can vouch that you don't have to just turn the TV on to see the world struggling. It's right in front of us. It's at work, beside us, in front of us, and behind us. Although it can be quite saddening, it's important that we maintain our strength and positive composure and compassionately reach out to others and embrace them and their own personal circumstance. Let them mirror what was once their hope and reassure their pride and dignity; exemplify humility and strength and perseverance and be mindful and thoughtful of others as they straddle their hurdles. Keep it as real and simple as you can. Let them know that it will all be good just by keeping it real and simple.

Listen to others. Don't just "hear" what people are saying. I was raised to say "yes sir" and "no sir" and "yes mam" and "no mam". And not a plain ole' "NO." Seriously? I listened all right, right down to the switches that swatted me into dancing around and learning respect. Those rose switches weren't plain ole' - they were thorny and hearty green in color and don't dare pluck the rotting brown ones. There would be no vanilla in your shake for quite a while. Yes, I'm a believer in an old fashioned spanking. We girls got our share of them. They (my sisters) should have gotten more because they used to shut me up in the bathroom (when I was a kid) in complete darkness and frantically laugh at me (from outside of course) while I stood screaming in the dark under the noisy overhead exhaust fan. It literally sounded like a jet was landing on me and it scared my britches off. That was so ugly but it's hilarious now. Childhood times are so meaningful and fun. Those were the good ole days and are what our tomorrows are made of. Keeping it real and simple was easier back then because we didn't know reality from simplicity. But when we grow up we must truly learn to simply keep things real to keep them really simple. It can be as hard or as easy as we make it sometimes.

Years back, after polishing-up my resume for online viewing, I realized there are many pertinent skills that we use in everyday life, whether it be professional or personal. We need to keep these sharpened. Although communication skills are a "must have" and first on my list, having excellent organizational skills can help our next day become a tremendous success. Take your e-mails for example (for those who need help in the organizing arena), simply set up folders in your list of contacts for home, insurance, phones, printer ink, etc... Be your own resource. Keeping it real and simple and organized will build structure and character and definitely diminish your stress level.

It is important to nurture and cherish our friendships, whether alive or dwindled, and learn not to burn bridges unnecessarily. Sometimes I hear from previous colleagues or run into someone I haven't seen in a while and it's nice to reflect upon the fact that our experiences were overall warm, polite and positive. Keep things real and simple and keep the horse in front of the carriage. Don't get too lost, distraught or overwhelmed with situations in which you will not easily be able to see the trees for the forest because you didn't keep a situation simple.

KEEP YOUR SNOW SHOVELS UP NORTH, BUFFALO

I have an awesome friend who lives in Buffalo. She and her husband are highly-regarded teachers in their school district where she teaches computer skills among other things. A long while ago, I was in a crunch when looking for a job. A recruiter (head-hunter) had contacted me about a very interesting position that matched my profile. It was a local job, but she didn't elaborate on very many details regarding the position for which I was interviewing. I was so tired of this kind of evasiveness. She was to send me a 5-part test on line (this was on a Sunday). The fifth test was on Excel and I told her I wasn't very familiar with this, that I had never used it and had never needed it. She instructed me to just do my best, but that I had to have an excellent score to proceed to the interview, set for the next day at 2:00pm. Seriously, bite me I thought, and send me $75 for this anguish! Being that I had a very limited amount of time to learn Excel, I took a quick online Excel tutorial and subsequently completed the 5 tests, the 5th one again being Excel.

The next morning, she informed me that I aced all of the tests except Excel. Seriously? My head ached. I had learned the formulas in Excel, and not just the simple basics like margins and settings. I didn't keep it simple because I couldn't see the trees from the huge forest. That morning, however, in an attempt to resume with my interview, she resent me the Excel test secretively, outlining where I, Clampett, went wrong. I called my "computer friend" in Buffalo and left her a quick voicemail explaining exactly what I needed. I didn't expect to hear from her, but guess what? My friend called me back promptly and made it simple. When she returned my call she had merely 7 minutes between classes to talk with me. Excel 101 it was. Shortly after retaking the test I went to my 2:00pm interview. I soon thereafter, proudly became President and CEO of Clampett-Enterprises, Inc. Actually it was all good by keeping it real and understanding simplicity.

POEM OF INSPIRATION

       I have a poem of inspiration that has hung on the wall of my office for many years. Its' message has truly helped me and many friends who have pursued the verse and felt its' meaning. The poem, "Sic Transit Gloria Mundi," is a Latin phrase meaning "Thus passes the glory of the world," and "worldly things are fleeting." For many years of momentarily inhaling these refreshing words while taking a few private moments to "regroup," I always assumed that the "Sic Transit Gloria Mundi" was a Middle Eastern poem. Well, we all know what "assuming" can make out of us, don't we? In any event, the poem flows as follows:

"This is the beginning of a new day. God has given me this

day to use as I will. I can waste it or use it for good. What

I do today is important because I'm exchanging a day of my

life for it. When tomorrow comes, this day will be gone forever,

 leaving something I have traded for it. I want it to be gain, not

loss; good, not evil; success, not failure; in order that I shall

not regret the price I paid for it."

       In all attempts to keep things "simple" I've found over the years that by merely taking a few steps back from things or situations (computers, televisions, etc.) that many times just simply unplugging the Clampett-item for 15 seconds will seriously save you more than just the "$75." If you get overwhelmed by an issue at task, step away from it for a few minutes and return to it. It's amazing how that works out most of the time and amazing how much frustration you have spared yourself. Breathe and keep it simple with a positive attitude. Have your chuckle for the day and embrace the simple things in life. Amen.

       With respect to keeping it simple and keeping things in perspective and in the right order, once again keeping that horse in front of the cart, understand your ultimate goals and objectives and exercise strategy, organization, and be less judgmental of others, ultimately accepting your cues from God. Try to find the prosperous path He has given you, and not the selfish one you've tried to create on your own. Keep things in perspective and maintain a positive attitude; one where others will feel your warm spirit and positivity and may potentially embrace it for their own well-being. Prioritize and focus on your objectives and establish your own personal boundaries, just as in teaching others how we want to be treated. Do unto others as we are instrumental in doing unto them. Once again, that door you opened for that elderly person may be the same door that someone opens for you some day. And, that some day could be tomorrow. We just never know. We shouldn't have to be faced with tragedy or turmoil to feel the heartache or pain in having to put our own feet in those shoes that have been worn and soiled.

JOB

As I speak of establishing and setting boundaries with others I am inclined to think of a business colleague with whom I had spent months training, over the phone, in the details of estate planning. Over time I came to realize that he was one of my "common denominator" friends and anticipated meeting him in person. We will call him "Job." Because we lived in separate states, Job and I had established a wonderful business and personal relationship over the phone. Outside of business, we found that we had a true musical background in common as well. He sent me downloads of his musical recordings over the internet which I found outstanding as he had done his "thing" in Nashville and truly knew his music. He desperately wanted to be geared in a different direction and the work I was training him for would become a priority. I understood that. Going through his devastating and unfortunate divorce and subsequently landing in the nurturing arms of the Salvation Army, I made arrangements for him to temporarily move in with me, under the pretension of him assisting me with my estate planning work. During this time I even entertained the thought of becoming his music agent, as he requested of me, but only after his work with me was coasting smoothly. That didn't happen.

During the time I had housed him, I quickly observed his work and prioritizing efforts were not conducive to the business ethics I had outlined. How could he learn this line of work while chatting online with ladies all day and night? In addition, his devious, yet failed attempts to enter into my locked office with his man-made skeleton keys made of paperclips that sometimes trailed along my hallway indicated his intrusive and underlying attempts to obtain personal information regarding my publishing companies... again, to no avail. I personally replaced my office door with a new lock. After a few verbal warnings and in observing that his focus was on socially playing music for entertainment and not working for a living, I ultimately had him escorted from my home. I didn't like doing so but I had given him many ultimatums. No work and all play makes Job a bye-bye boy.

NEGATIVITY VS. POSITIVITY

I have found that in many years of working in the corporate world, while wearing the suits, heels, and stockings (and by the way whoever created pantyhose needs to be popped upside the head) that I have always relied upon a repetition in my simple everyday prayers to God; "PLEASE LEAD, GUIDE, AND DIRECT ME TO HAPPINESS AND SUCCESS." Many friends have called me over the years, sometimes with philosophical or spiritual questions for discussion. One that sticks out in my mind is when a friend asked me recently if I knew that we should always be careful what we "ask " for? I answered him with my opinion that we should also CUSHION ourselves for whatever the answer may be.

I've noticed that when people have distinct concerns, problems, or worries, they frequently go to a boatload of friends (hence a lot of opinions) for advice that sometimes ultimately causes confusion. Truly know who your personal counselors are and that God is there at all times. We've all heard that less is more... less negativity in your life results in more positivity in it. Less drama in your life will harvest more emotional freedom in your warm path. The less bitterness and judgment that we are faced with can lead us to having more ease and warmth in our strides in life and finding more humor in it in lieu of anxiety. Keeping a simpler life and having perhaps less stressful responsibilities, including relationships, can be the tip of an iceberg to overall contentment and solitude. Additionally, and perhaps more importantly, once again I've found it essential to weed out those "acquaintances" who you thought were your friends... the ones who have caused you anguish, bitterness, worry, etc., over and over again and cause problems in your world with their dramatic and sometimes ludicrous and/or backstabbing ways. I've never ever had those types of friends...not in many years that I can recall. I'm just saying...I know they are out there, ready to suck you into their whirlwind of a life just as a tornado sucks in everything in its' path and turns it to devastation.

I've found that having a handful of trustworthy friends who have proven what friendship is all about and value and respect their "word" in itself is a true blessing. These friends should be cherished and held onto forever. These types of proven friends are irreplaceable, and true friends are hard to find. "Weeding out the old with the new" is a great logic to familiarize ourselves with and understand as we walk this precious journey and gift of life, especially if it involves our happiness, integrity and overall health and peace. As I advise many friends, keep the ball in your court and make wise shots and be a good sport regardless of the outcome. Weeding through your personal acquaintances when evaluating who your true friends (BFFs) are is similar to getting an insurance quote on a claim. Obtain three quotes, make your sound evaluation and be done with it. Get it off your plate and enjoy your day. Avoid confusion in dealing with multitudes of opinions and situations. Keep it real and simple.

JUDGEMENT

In my experience, it is a pleasure to assist folks with their estate planning. But sometimes people simply say "we have the software to do that." Seriously? Do they use their software to buy their home or to have their car repaired or tonsils removed? Probably not, but that is their prerogative. Period. It's just my job to make suggestions and not to pass judgment. In other words, it's their plate to tend to, not mine. Once again, their pillow and their mirror and not my business. However, it's important that folks remember, like back in the old days, if you hand-drafted a legal document yourself (such as your last will and testament) on a sheet of toilet paper, then shared it with 10 different people, how many versions of that draft do you think you would get? Ten of course. People get things so twisted. Do things the right way, and do them correctly by taking your time while exercising good judgment.

Knowing that we can only do so much with what we have in front of us at any given time can help rationalize our decision-making endeavors. Stay keen and sharp by keeping focused, prioritizing, and bettering yourself in every way possible. Be frugal; exercise your wisdom and positive energies and enlighten our younger entrepreneurs by educating them how they can gain the same strength, and experience the same freedoms in life; and share their inherited wisdom with their loved ones by practicing the simple fundamentals this sisterhood of America and God's creation was built upon.

No project is accomplished overnight. Utilize the strengths that you found instrumental in the development of your professional and personal growth. Take time for yourself and reflect on where you are, where you've been, and most importantly, where you want to be. Take your cues from God, position yourself accordingly, keeping your faith and never stay too busy for God's direction and guidance. If you're too busy for yourself, you'll stay lost, going around and around on that rat wheel. God is never too busy for us, and we should never be too busy for Him.

Whether you may or may not be able to worship in the spiritual sanctity of a church, let your faith in God be your personal sanctuary wherever you are, in your physical existence and where your faith lay. Whether it be your home, office, or a sandy beach, make your sanctuary YOUR personal sanctuary with no disturbances or judgments; again, in your own solitude wherever you may be. And always remember tne important thing; wherever you go, there you are...keep things real and keep them as simple as possible. Keep high-stepping with strong strides into your ambitious tomorrow and don't backstroke into your yesterdays. Take time off from work and away from the turmoil, drama, obstacles and headaches many of us are faced and challenged with in our every day life. In doing so, you may rebound with a vital and rejuvenating sensation, not to mention a more positive perspective and attitude in your journey by merely keeping your glass half full and not half empty. Enjoy and respect yourself as well as others and escape from your pool of exhaustion. Know that when you give and give and give, you will probably be expected to give even more at some point and time down the road. Your energies may ultimately weaken and seemingly become annihilated if you don't begin setting stronger boundaries. Again, set your boundaries and limitations with pride and dignity and an abundance of strength and courage. There's nothing wrong with being somewhat eccentric once in a while; you may find that it builds character and perhaps respect. Uniqueness. People will respect the effort you put into yourself and understand that your self-assurance is powered by strength, spirit, warmth, and positivity. And also by the wonderful, powerful grace of God. Inasmuch as there are a lot of control freaks roaming around, little do they know who is truly in control and that we will all face our creator one day- at any given time. And the creator is not them.

Some folks may acquire a twisted opinion that you are cocky, but that may be their personal interpretation of the word "confident" as a result of their glass always being half empty and not half full, like you tend to keep yours. Folks tend to get quite intimidated and/or envious of confident people, especially when you might be trying to better yourself and are successful at it. Bottom line is that they need to focus and tend to their own plate and not yours. I'm not being judgmental here, just merely factual. Ultimately, it is THEIR pillow that they must sleep on every night and not yours. Right? It is indeed THEIR mirror they must look into ever day. And if they feel worthy of hugging themselves in that reflection, then may they please do so. Again, it's THEIR mirror, and not YOURS that they need to be concentrating on and hugging, and THEIR plate that needs to be tended to, not YOURS. Once again, tend to your own plate, sleep on your own pillow, and hug yourself in the mirror each day if you feel worthy of that hug. It's quite simple.

In the same logic, do people understand that when they are pointing their

43

finger of judgment at someone else, there are also three fingers pointing back at them? Get off of everyone else and concentrate on YOU and those fingers of judgment pointing back at you will no longer do so. Again, it's your own pillow that you sleep on at night, and it's your own mirror that you face. Again, give yourself warm hugs if you feel worthy of facing yourself in your reflection. Give yourself tremendous hugs because lots of folks fail to see themselves as being a dynamic person and many folks are too selfish to extend gratitude to that person and let them simply know how fantastic they really are. Once again, tend to your own plate and not the Jones' next door. Simply being factual and not judgmental here, I encourage folks to go purchase some new plated China to tend to or simply go and get a Clampett-ass job or hobby. There's way too much judgment going on in this world I've noticed. It gets quite exhausting seeing people looking down their noses and judging others and focusing on someone else's world rather than their own, while energetically judging the other instead of utilizing their time and energy to focus on themselves. Judge not that ye be not judged. I don't think God created step ladders for those high horses, did he? Actually, there is probably a website for something like that...perhaps at www.getoveryourself.com?

EMMA

My aforementioned friend, Emma (who lives in Buffalo, NY) and I have been friends for over 15 years. I've had the pleasure of personally meeting her only once, yet we converse as often as our busy schedules allow. She has indeed been one of my "common denominator" friends. I've watched her sons grow over the years despite the distance we live from each other, and have been proud and applauded her in her personal and professional growth and journey in life. She is quite iconic in her community and family and needless to say is highly regarded and respected by her friends, family, and colleagues. She used to call me years ago when her kids were toddlers and throwing car keys in the toilet, laughing and crying in the same moment, while making repeated attempts to get a handle on things. Thanks for sharing... love them but glad they are yours... Your $75 is so in the mail. To merely "get away" for a week she flew to North Carolina many years ago and we had a chock-full blast of fun, travel, adventure and excitement. We drove to the gorgeous city of Charleston, SC which is a beautiful southern historical landmark. I wanted to take her to the deeper south because she'd never been to the southern states and I wanted her to make that warm discovery as well as ascertain that she didn't have things twisted-- that we Southerners ain't got only 3 real teeth in our pie-hole down here; that we don't hang out all day long in smokey pool halls or lay around on trashy sofas laden with nicotine, straddled on the confines of the sizzling front porch of our caved-in mobile home while slamming empty beer cans against our gambling foreheads, playing dueling banjos, while eating fresh watermelon and spitting seeds through the gaps of our front teeth which had never been properly introduced to one another-- and trying to out-drink each other under our starry milky way while listening to our favorite Hee-Haw tunes with Roy and Buck- or that our only dilapidated car of rusted bolts resting on concrete cinder-blocks in our front yard is our only hope and dream of getting somewhere or make something out of our life.

Many Northerners perhaps, have the opinion that we all have marijuana plants growing out of a used toilet bowl in our front yard, or a tomato plant growing out of the wheel barrow beside it, I needed to convey that we are not all Jed Clampett-hillbillies, blowing slobbering jolts of Clampett-rhythm into smelly whiskey jugs while tapping our Clampett-ass feet, and that most of us don't literally wear pigtails and

45

flaunt around in a skimpy red and white flannel top. My grandma stopped that trend decades ago. I'm just saying...I love the Clampetts. They laughed their way to the bank a few times as I remember. One has to have a sense of humor. My Yankee friend thought none of this nonsense and felt the south was a different, yet seemingly pleasurable experience for her. Seriously though, some people do get twisted ideas in their heads. While she was here, I did introduce her to some of our southern, traditional and tasty staples like boiled peanuts, grits and fried green maters; not at one time, and not in that order. She did admit that eating like that just makes "ya wanna slap ya mamma." "Slap ya mamma" is merely a southern phrase used when folks are enjoying their food, and maybe enjoying it way too much. Hallelujah and pass the gravy!

Whether it be to a friend, colleague, and/or family member, always demonstrate and be a positive influence to others to the best of your ability. Reflect that God is your primary resource if you want to experience the fruitfulness of the world we walk upon and "The Word" that we should live by. The Heaven that we'll ultimately be called into will be much less cumbersome, yielding glorious mountains and valleys, than those we struggle through on earth; and will provide the eternal warmth and comfort that most lost souls are lonely for and in search of.

MY PARENTS-THE ROCK OF FAITH

My parents exemplified structure not only by being strong, loving, caring, responsible, and accountable, but also by demonstrating a self-confident yet compassionate composure. Their nature to influence everyone to be their best- with encouragement- not only to and for their own children, but also the broader realm of family and community- the many people they have acquired respect from, and being well deserved- by simply being the Christian iconic role models and soldiers in society and our entire family of close relatives. They have portrayed and exercised through their leadership skills the simple tactics that we seldom have the honor of experiencing these days whether it be family or politics. As a nation, I feel we may need to perhaps reevaluate the fundamentals of Ms. America's future as we do our own personal goals and missions. Be mindful to be selfless and understand that not everything is about you. Keep a check in the mirror and by all means hug yourself daily. Keep it real and keep it simple. It will all be good, through God.

Speaking of my "Pop," I used to get so upset when he was seemingly overly insistent and impatient while waiting for me to get ready for church. Trying to get pretty, and doing hair and makeup, is not just a quick shower and a shave as some men may see it. Twas more than just the smell of a nice fragrance. The "getting ready" is a process for us gals... we were always early to arrive anyway, and the church wasn't going anywhere. He was just instilling punctuality and perhaps authority in my mind's eye. Such treasured attributes. I can still jokingly visualize the hopes of one day witnessing a man struggling with having to strap nylons over his big calves while lying on his bed, struggling like a spider to stretch them ornately and tightly around his legs and then dash to the car without breaking a heel or getting a "run" in his hose, all the while stroking that last dab of lipstick on. I would love to see that one! If you've ever seen Mel Gibson in " What Women Want" you know exactly what I mean. In any event, I had my own car back then. It was simple.

Even though I struggled to get those stupid pantyhose on, he was the boss and if I had to go to Sunday school with one eye painted and one not, it was what it was and I obeyed. Is the word "obeyed" even used these days? He was the teacher and leader of simple instruction and direction—how to work and get paid for chores, simply washing his car and scrubbing the whitewalls of his tires very flawlessly, doing things right the very first time, and making sure the lawn was manicured as I promised to after contractually negotiating with him. Keeping things real and simple, it was always good, somehow, but always through the grace of God.

He taught us honor, pride, self-esteem, endurance, integrity, prioritizing, focusing and simple respect and courtesy. We respected what he'd worked so hard for to provide for his family and I, in return, hugged him back for his perseverance. Respect. Honor. Value. They taught us the world by teaching us the values and fundamentals of life- understanding and acknowledging the foundation that we were to walk on through the work and grace of God. Years ago when they moved, what seemed to be a zillion miles from me, I swore that I would not ever take the "convenience of seeing my parents" for granted. Not just that, but not taking ANYTHING at all for granted, the first breath of air we wake up to each day, the pillow that we lay on, the mirror we look into every day and even the running water we wash our face with, and not even the trees it takes to make the checks for the $75 for putting up with your Clampett-ass every day. That is just not part of who they taught me to be.

THANKFULNESS

Thank someone for simply shining a new color to your everyday rainbow. Simply said, notice something special in others instead of always shouting your own self to them (otherwise known as tooting your own horn). So often, a humble person needs a warmer hug than you may perhaps be giving. Stay humble and thank God for your many blessings. Thank Him for each day and each moment you are awake and for every relaxing moment in the comforts of your day. Simply keep it real, and simple and remember it's all good through God. Just keep it all good to expect that it will be all good.

Sometimes we have to take a few steps backwards to take a few steps forward in an attempt to figure out why we're on a hamster wheel, where we are on it, why we are on it, and how to jump off of it somehow. As it goes around and around, don't get too dizzy, just keep your perspective, knowing that through your faith and confidence in God there can and will be a brighter tomorrow. Take your heavy stumbling blocks that you've walked upon and turn them into stepping stones, gliding into a more promising, spirited, and hopeful tomorrow, while keeping a positive attitude with each stride. Remember, the sun is always out, we just simply can't always see it. There is usually a message in the messes we encounter; we just need to identify them with acknowledgment, accountability and rectification and turn that mess into a message.

Treat yourself without guilt and limit your emotional availability from everyone else's problems, 24/7. Again, set your boundaries with grace and dignity, not by someone else's expectations. Your blood pressure is important to your family, believe it or not, and your body will thank you.

LET GO AND LET GOD

Turn your radio up once in a while and simply shake your booty. It's OK to have fun when you feel like high-stepping it in your own element. Life is too short not to cut loose once in a while; cut that rug and tear it up! Remember that you are in your own pilot seat, but acknowledging that God can truly navigate your wheel of life will indeed get you to your destination and into the direction you desire. Life is very short... Yesterday I was 5 and when I woke up this morning, I was 90.

Speak with pleasantries in your voice even when you're calling about an incorrect bill you received. Being nice and pleasant will take you places. You don't have to sound like a cheerleader or Hitler when you are calling about that bill, and it's not the customer service rep's fault that their computer system sucks. Let customer service folks know when they are doing a great job and that they are really good at what they do. It's really not that hard. Seriously, they'd probably rather pay your $75 bill to get your ugly attitude off the phone than to deal with it. Take time to smile a little harder sometimes, and once again, simply hold the door open for someone. Try to keep things about others rather than making everything about yourself.

My sister Terry used to tell me to simply "get over the dumb stuff" (putting it nicely) and don't let pettiness get you upset. Deal with it, toss it out or whatever so that your energies are not exhausted. Simply let it go. Your ability to "let it go" will show to others if you let it...and so will your positivity. People love to hear and see your smile and to even feel your passion when you just simply hug them during an intimate conversation over the phone. Just simply "let it go and let God" and all will be good.

MOM'S TEACHINGS

Our Mom taught so much more than she'll ever know, not only to us girls, but to my numerous cousins who were also learning from our elders. Exemplifying her strength and endurance and setting her boundaries with love and compassion and most importantly, her strength and her faith in our Lord. No one could ever dream of having a better mother than the one I am blessed with. Simply staying extremely strong and organized was one of the largest, most crucial fundamentals I realized as a child. In my young days, the observant brat that I was, I noticed how things "worked" with the older folks whom I highly respected and regarded.

Whether it be my Mom in the kitchen or my Pop in his organized garage with everything at the reach of a calculated glance, there was always a lesson to be learned. My Mom would take me shopping from store to store, being frugal to save a penny whenever possible, by shopping on triple or quadruple coupon day. I was like, seriously? She was taking care of our family. It was all about being frugal of course. I watched her over the years, feeding the 5 of us with awesome southern cooking, washing pots one after another while preparing an entire meal. Mom kept the whole method of cooking and cleaning dishes through the entire process and by the time she was through with this incredible meal, there was hardly a dish to wash. She kept it real and simple.

STAYING ORGANIZED

Stay organized. Don't veer away from what you know works for you, regardless. Stay focused. Look around and observe. Don't get caught up in the confusion of other's habits or even their business. Take care of your plate and focus on yourself. The opposing logic tends to use a lot of energy. As a reminder, it's your cushioned pillow that you must sleep on every night, and once again it's that same mirror you must face every day. Hugs!

Don't ever underestimate yourself. Take your history, your methodology, and start connecting the dots to your present element and that which you anticipate. In essence, I learned this by simply taking a deep breath and connecting the traits of who has helped me in the past, in the present, and knowing who my resources are for current and future development. An important component to remember is to never be too prideful in shaking the hand of someone while walking up that corporate ladder- and shake it with strength and respect because once again, you never know when you'll have to shake that same hand on the way back down that same ladder. Keep things real. It is what it is, always.

Be your own resource and make things happen. Don't count on others to make your life complete. First of all, finding God is the simple fundamental of spirit, success and overall happiness and eternity. Without God, it cannot be simple, and it won't be "all good." Life with God can be "all good."

We need to remember that God has a purpose for each of us and we need to be open-minded and very mindful of His power and powerful "cues" or "clues" and to simply achieve our goals which can lead to prosperity, wealth and overall happiness and success. Not rich in gems, but rich in simple happiness. Don't underestimate yourself or God's power. Don't ever feel like you're less than perfect. Again, go give yourself a hug in your mirror and don't forget to SEE yourself. We all question Him- we are only human. Remember God has a sense of humor and so should we, once in a while.

A SENSE OF HUMOR

Speaking of going through life without having a sense of humor, many years ago I worked for a large patenting corporation and sat in a cubicle, located within eye contact of a lot of passing, busy, furious, yet sometimes hilarious people. They could always see that I stayed focused on my computer work- not studying them for a second unless they were "something" to look at—like the tall, dark, and handsome golfer who made me smile many times. A very large dictionary laid resting on the opposite wall of my cubicle, opened-Bible style for use by several departments. One day a very snooty woman (who quite frankly no one liked because she ate sour lemons all the time) came flaring by and busily looked up a word, like she didn't have time to be learning the spelling of a new word. Without looking up at her eyeballs I calmly asked her what word she couldn't find. She replied indignantly to me the word as if I knew where this country was, and without pause I calmly replied the spelling of "CZECHOSLOVAKIA." I thought "bite me" and where's my $75? Go polish off the rest of your lemons. In other words, it doesn't pay off to be so sour.

REFLECTION

Throughout our journey in life, it's important that we take time to reflect. Ponder the path you've walked and be mindful of the journey you're excelling in. Taking mental and spiritual time for yourself is the best $75 you'll ever want to spend. Keep it simple, and shower others with warmth and spirit and see how many pennies will show up. Reflecting and being mindful of your past experiences whether they be good or bad will help keep your tomorrow in perspective. Know that regardless, you are special. Be your own resource for everything that you possibly can, but reach out when you need to. How many people have asked you for favors? Over and over again. If it's the same one with the same favors simply send them a bill for $75.

Make things happen in your life and don't expect others to make it happen for you. Keep things real and simple knowing that "it is what it is" and that you can only do so much with what you have at the moment. Through vision and thought and your strength and faith in God, you can make things happen not only for yourself, but in the world as well. We can't simply sit around anticipating positive changes. Make things happen. Your smile will be endless and so should the reflection in your mirror. Give yourself a hug.

Praise God every day wherever your sanctuary is. Thank the firefighters who saved lives on 911. Understand that just because you don't play a musical instrument or cannot read or write or talk, that you DO have a talent (sometimes called the "fruit of the spirit") which is special and unique unto you. Understand that you have touched someone in your own personal way through the warm, infinite spirit of God's grace and glory.

SATURDAY'S PHONE CALLS

My mom and I have our special morning chats on the phone on Saturdays and I always look forward to hearing her voice and talking about life while laughing and feeling her pleasant and friendly, motherly spirit which has always filled me with warmth and positive energy. We were talking recently and I told her that I had a cookout the night before and had entertained several friends by blissfully playing the piano. I didn't realize how long it had been since I had enjoyed festivity so much. My friendly guests/neighbors weren't aware that I enjoy playing music or that I even owned a piano. We had a really great time. Mom revealed the fact that she was so pleased to see me back in my musical element that had always made me smile and feel happy and vibrant. Being that she doesn't play a musical instrument other than playing many songs using only the black keys on the piano (which is absolutely hilarious) she meekly said "Vic, I always wondered what my talent was..."). At that very moment I was absolutely stunned and without hesitation, stood up like a proud peacock pacing the floor, and chuckled, "Mom, your talent is that you are the BEST MOM, AND BEST FRIEND AND BEST WIFE AND BEST SISTER AND NEIGHBOR AND AUNT that anyone could EVER imagine having and please don't ever forget that." She is a rock, just like Pop. However, I'd prefer to regard the dynamic duo as a mountain in lieu of a rock. She's quite shorter than I am and she will occasionally come up to me smiling and point upward to me saying, "You may be taller than me, but you know who the boss is"! I hug her and say thank you Lord with warmth, spirit and a gracious appreciation. I wanted to tell her that her check for $75 zillion was in the mail. It's in the same envelope with Pop's, as well as Terry's and Karen's.

Our parents are our structural backbone and the true source of our dignity. Let your special people know how immeasurable they are and learn from their positive energy, fellowship, guidance, frugality, faith, structure, discipline, wisdom, advice, encouragement and appreciation as they demonstrate and live their life.

Mark a memorable indention on your family tree and treasure it with satin gloves. Again, hear that simple little prayer "Dear Lord, please lead, guide and direct me into happiness and success." It's that simple if you truly mean it. Let God be the pilot on your hamster wheel and He will help get you off of the rat wheel you may feel

that you're riding. Traveling around and around at a fast pace will only make you dizzy!
Keep things real and as simple as possible. Did you know that it takes a lot more
energy to frown rather than simply smile? In other words, folks would much rather see
you standing upright instead of standing on your Clampett-head all the time. I'm just
saying...

FL AS IN FLORIDA

A short time ago, I was contacted via phone by someone who was actually responding to my internet inquiry pertaining to running a home-based business. I was so glad to hear from her. Being that I have many friends, colleagues and acquaintances, I will refer to her as "FL" as in the sunny state where she lives. She and her husband and their beautiful daughters have a home-based business in the travel industry, and being family-oriented, I was enthralled to hear about and relate to their professional testimony and was eager to hear what they had to share. By putting her God-given spirit and guidance into sharing their success stories (over a period of time), I was introduced to a realm of spiritual magnitude and fellowship which I felt could or would possibly lead into continuing to build my professional development and personal gratification. She had simply suggested that I attend an upcoming seminar that was going to be held in DC, hosted by the famous Dani Johnson. It was a great idea I thought, but I felt it quite impossible to afford that immediate funding as my overhead expense budget was already exhausted at that particular time. However, after taking a long dance with Peter and Paul, while simply trying to actually find a Peter to pay Paul, I was determined to find a way to fund this workshop and the accommodations thereof. I also had to do some homework. I'd been conversing about this particular travel industry with various professionals via telecom over an extended period of time and I'd already known who the very famous Dani Johnson was. That in itself was a seller.

I very diligently tried to work the trip into my work schedule and budget. I wanted to attend this particular exciting upcoming seminar in DC because this one in particular was going to be the closest one to me, geographically, for quite some time. It therefore didn't take long to set aside any skepticism (and I indeed did my homework with regards to the travel industry) and made my way to attend the seminar in DC which I knew would be vital to my continued business development and integrity.

I had been communicating with FL and another professional acquaintance in Canada over a period of months and had established a very warm, trusting, God-spirited and encouraging relationship with them. They simply encouraged me to attend this seminar/workshop to enhance and perhaps reevaluate my overall professional, personal, and spiritual comfort. Everyone needs a self-check once in a while. God bless them for having such faith in me. FL knew that I had a lot on my plate with my existing estate planning work and that I was wearing many hats. But she also knew that I had a vision and there was simply a puppy on my plate and I had begun to feel like the hamster on the rat wheel. Making keen, accurate, prompt business decisions for other companies is what my professional background entailed so when she SIMPLY and smilingly advised me over the phone to "practice what I preach" I simply told her to "bite me" and we both cracked up. Game on I thought....seriously? Her passion for others, faith in God, encouragement, wisdom and guidance will always be cherished. What an outstanding family I had already truly grown to love and so looked forward to meeting.

After eventually finding a Peter to pay Paul, I made rapid arrangements to get to the seminar in DC, which a month earlier I had wanted to attend in Dallas, TX. I was not about to let this opportunity pass me by. Not this time. In lieu of making a long drive in such a tired stage, I decided to take a bus to DC and relax, and utilize the internet service while traveling, in an attempt to work, communicate with some of my clients and the few folks that needed to know where I was, and to let them know that I was okay during this journey. I had not only my laptop on this journey, but a briefcase, pocketbook, sack of groceries and what felt like a 200 pound suitcase (we women certainly know how to travel with our closet)! Thank God for yard work and trying to stay halfway fit.

Traveling on the upper level of the bus, I warmly anticipated meeting the beautiful people who had encouraged me to make such a very wise decision to attend this extremely motivational seminar. The folks from FL and Canada did not have a picture of me because I am private and remain distant from Facebook. I however, had been forwarded pictures of them and could not wait to meet them or at least have a chance of recognizing them at the seminar.

Upon arriving at the bus terminal in DC, there was a penny at my foot. Seriously? I laughed and pocketed it. Terry's spirit was present I felt...exactly what I'd always heard- that pennies around you are indicative that there is a spirit around you, one that is not necessarily haunting, but one that is peacefully surrounding and guiding you in existence with love, compassion and faith. My sister was indeed the shiny penny from Heaven and had been for quite some time. What an overwhelming discovery it had become and always brought a joyful smile to my face. Over a period of several years, the number of pennies I'd found throughout my house in such absolutely strange locations became quite uncanny. Especially when I subsequently heard what some folks found that was indicative of-once again- a spiritual presence.

After several attendants at Union Station tried to assist me in their seemingly lame attempts of passing the buck, and upon observing that no one knew where they were or who they were, I wanted to extend my hand into the air and simply ask, "If there is anyone in this Union Station who is not on drugs, would you please raise your hand"? I truly wonder how many hands I would have seen. No wonder politics is what it is sometimes- no offense to anyone.

FL had called me several times during all this crazy turmoil; me feeling like an over-heated camel with " miles to go before I sleep" and being groped by underground shuttle drunkards trying to figure out who I was with so many bags. They literally had one glassy eye open. All four of mine were wide open. Apart from the aggravation and exhaustion, it was actually quite comical. But hearing from FL had truly kept my spirit and momentum going and she made me smile as always. So here I was, in DC, hauling heavy baggage and exhausted of this ridiculous nonsense during my journey. I just simply wanted to get to the hotel. Furthermore, it was getting to be very late at night and I recall that the underground escalators had already been shut off.

Power housing up those numerous, halted flights of steps became more tolerable when I finally started hearing the glorious sounds of the honking horns of taxi cabs, I presumed and hoped for. At that point, I didn't care who was honking their horn as long as it had wheels and an air conditioner and could get me to the hotel. Keep in mind that this trip was arranged at the last minute and it would probably be the last one of the like as far as travel goes, no pun intended. But FL was extremely supportive and motivated my endurance and strength and reminded me of what my journey was all about...which was simply attending a powerful, motivational seminar and learning from it. It was also very interesting that I kept continuously finding an abundance of pennies lying on the ground...I wasn't really looking for them at all but I'm just saying... I'm not studying that one, but it was what it was and I truly did feel spirited comfort and encouragement around me. I was quite ready to park my camel with all of my luggage hanging off my sweaty, weary humps and exchange it for a Georgia work mule. Then shoot it. The work mule, that is.

It was 12:00 midnight and there was no one in the shuttle area by the upper level ticket booth when I miraculously stumbled upon a female and a male parking attendant. What a God send! At that moment I dropped my bags and simply asked (after taking a deep breath and bending over to regain my composure) " WOULD SOMEONE PLEASE CALL ME A CAB"? With just a mere glance at them I could tell they were warm, spirited folks who, by their radiance gave me air hugs. The very kind, welcoming lady said "Girlfriend- you look absolutely exhausted, and I HAVE YOUR BACK." While she promptly communicated with the nearby cabby, the kind gentleman approached me stating "And I've got our bags, Mam." Within seconds, she said, " the cab is waiting for you girlfriend and he has his a/c turned up for you." Smiling, I said " Girlfriend, you rock. THANK YOU SO MUCH." While walking away, I turned and asked, "MAM, WHAT IS YOUR NAME"? She smiled and said "GAIL, girlfriend, which means VOICE OF JOY- AND THAT'S WHY I'M HERE RIGHT NOW FOR YOU." Without giving her a sermon I laughed and said "It's all good- thank your for keeping it real and simple and SPREADING YOUR JOY. YOU ARE A BEAUTIFUL GRACE FROM GOD."

The male attendant was so sweet with helping me cart my bags from that tunnel, which reminded me of the long stroll through the tunnel in the old football/Coke commercial. He was so warm and kind and he really felt my aggravation and exhaustion. As he so kindly nestled me into the cab, I said "Thank you so much for your kindness." As I handed him a tip, he declined it saying, "seriously"? and instructed the cabby to take care of me. Before I left and thanked him, I turned and said "Sir, what is your name"? looking deeply into his eyes. He said "Terry." I said "God bless you Terry," while smiling and graciously giving him a warm hug. I was in such awe as I could feel the presence of my own sister, Terry, and her confidence in my present endeavor.

I sat in the back seat of the air conditioned cab and simply handed the cabby a printout of my directions and address to the Hyatt Hotel. It seemed like it had taken 20 hot hours to get to. The driver was a pleasant, warm Iranian gentleman who knew I was not about to engage in "out-of-state tourist cab driving" games. We had a nice conversation as he simply drove me to the entrance door of the hotel, and not around the state of Virginia. Scrounging to get money from my pocket to pay him, I began thanking him for being so courteous and honest. Before exiting the cab, with humor and hesitation, I just had to ask his name. By this time, I knew there was some kind of pattern trending through the air, and I couldn't wait for this one. In his pleasant, Iranian accent, he told me his name. I didn't quite get it so I sat up at attention and said "I'm sorry, what's your name again"? I repeated it back to him the way I heard it projected to me (i.e.. Testa what?). He repeated his name once again, and I said "Your name is TESTIFY"? He said "yes Mam." I chuckled my camel self into the hotel after thanking him and practically threw $75 to him. The pennies from Heaven, the voice of glory, the presence of Terry and a testimony. I've never encountered such a unique combo from a sandwich shop, much less this surprising unique one. I knew at that point that I may be led into a different direction than what I had intended. It was important to stay open-minded and focused and that's exactly what I did.

IT'S FINALLY "DOWN TIME"

The hotel had reserved me a somewhat private room because I had asked not to be disturbed. My computer/work etc. was with me at all times. After sleeping a mere 3 hours and communicating with FL, I approached the seminar the next day alerting folks as to their inquiry of what I was wearing. Upon registration, FL and I made our very warm personal introduction. Without my knowledge, she so simply and kindly guided me to the front of the line where she had stood in for me. She then snapped my picture, got my signature and made it all good for me through the grace of God. Hallelujah and Amen.

The seminar was initially for 2 days but I was highly advised and encouraged by Canada and FL to attend a third day for a VITAL workshop that would help me experience and be knowledgeable of how to achieve spiritual and perhaps financial freedom through leadership, spirit, courage and testimony. Being that I had registered late, I was an attendee in the "overflow" room and viewed the seminar on the large screen. With only 3 hours of sleep, I'd ironically never felt so inspired, spirited, and full of energy as I did that day. Enthralled, I left the overflow room that evening after pounding out a novel of mental and hand-written notes. And then, upon exiting the aisle, as I departed, I glanced down at the reflection of something shiny on the floor and couldn't believe the presence I found. The penny was even heads-up. This was the most brilliant, dynamic, powerful, educational, innovative, spirited, motivational, and authentic seminar I had ever been graced with attending and I will gladly be a testament to the wealth of knowledge and leadership skills I gained in hopes of sharing with others someday. Hats off to you, Dani and Hans!

There were 2 Hyatt hotels side by side and I stayed in the smaller one. The large one was a brief 5 minute walk away and was where the seminar was held. I indeed made the spontaneous last minute decision to attend the workshop on the third day and was faced with having to find a vacant room for that particular night as my existing hotel room had already been booked. After finally making plans to room with someone at the other Hyatt, I was simply lounging in the lobby waiting for the shuttle to pick me and my camel and luggage up, dressed in my business attire of course, when a lady entered the lobby and snobbishly looked down at me and said "

I'm in room 312 and I have 4 pillows in my room that need to be fluffed"! I chuckled as I glanced up at her and said "Okay, but do I look like a pillow fluffer to you"? She hesitantly remarked, "actually, you look like you own the place."   I replied that "looks can be deceiving" as I proceeded to gather a pillow on a cart nearby and showed her how to fluff it herself. Needless to say, I was SO glad to eventually park my camel back in the Queen City of North Carolina.

KNOWING RATHER THAN SEEING

Sometimes when we make time to focus on where we WANT to be instead of where we've been, we will find that people who KNOW us rather than just simply "SEE" us will have the most valuable confidence and support in and for us. Embrace these people and shower them with warmth and gratitude. Keep things real and simple and invest $75 or so for "where you want to be". It will all be good.

I frequently have lengthy conversations with a select few friends. One cheerful, sunny afternoon, while relaxing and having a nice phone conversation with a dear friend on my patio, which was located underneath the big, tall, leafy Oak trees, I noticed several humongous squirrel nests lodged in the huge limbs above. The squirrels were prepping their young because Fall was soon approaching and I found it to be quite intriguing. I was glad they had created a warm spot to keep their nuts and keep their babies warm until I looked down on my lawn and noticed that the cotton lining of my grill cover and my chair cushions had been extracted. My warmth quickly dissipated to the edge of cold. Those scoundrels! Where was my freaking $75 you little fatties? Some folks would have shot them and made squirrel stew out of them or maybe even thrown them onto the grill. My preference is grilled chicken. Those little ones needed a home, so my home became theirs, for a while, and I was glad I could be of assistance to them.

COUNT YOUR BLESSINGS

Throughout the many years of making estate planning presentations, I began to notice how truly blessed I am while recognizing how families have literally and unfortunately broken apart while going through probates issues. It was just as difficult to witness these fragile issues...as it was to witness an elderly lady in a nursing home literally throw up through her nose while sitting in her wheelchair.

Years ago, after prepping for one of my estate planning appointments, I met with a wonderful, wonderful man to have his legal documents prepared. He was a quadriplegic and after a life-alternating meeting with him (from my perspective) he began to sign his documents with a pen in his mouth. Apparently he'd done this in his past, but this was here, this was now, and this was with me, sitting by his side. I go "by the book" with regard to my work ethics, but I know how to roll with margin, and help people feel dignified, all while being legal and respectful. I gently took the pen from his mouth and handled the closing process accordingly. Fighting back my tears and hugging him, I noticed (as I had already, for all intensive legal purposes) all of the monitors he had hanging inside and outside- watching every inch and motion of any action in and/or around his humble abode- capturing and nurturing every ounce of support, love and strength and hopes of continued survival from his close family and friends. He also happened to be a musician and had an incredible array of musical instruments and equipment which sparkled my eyes. Musical instruments! I just wanted to pull a Barbara Mandrel and do a happy dance after seeing and feeling all of the joy and fellowship and musical love and bond with his family, and hearing their musical, harmonic praises. I thought what a blessing it was to meet him and his loving family, full of spirit, praise and gratitude. It had been quite some time since I had felt so much spirit in someone else's home...their sanctuary. They kept it real, and they kept it simple; knowing that it was indeed all good, through God.

MY office had also assigned me to yet another challenging appointment. This one was also quite delicate in that the older gentleman I was to meet with was on oxygen. It was our practice to always personally call these folks prior to their appointment to ascertain their competency in these circumstances. The wife who retrieved my call was so nice on the phone and was pleased that I, being a female (duly noted) was meeting them at their home. She was so sweet and made me chuckle when she implied she'd put her teeth in for our visit.

I met with the elegant lady, teeth and all, and their wonderful caregiver who I knew after a quick minute needed her documents prepared as well. Prior to the caregiver leaving, I obtained the required information and instructed the Mrs. to make sure her husband was presentable for me to enter their bedroom, as he lay resting. She left me alone at the kitchen table momentarily and I briefly chatted with the pleasant caregiver. I did not know at that time how much I would be in communication with her later. Shortly after, the caregiver left. It was then that I heard the shrieking scream of my name and I ran to the bedroom while urgently positioning my cell phone in my hand to dial 911. The Mr. was clearly having an extreme convulsion and was grotesquely urinating everywhere. As I called the medics, I tried to calm this beautiful, older woman down. I held and consoled her, as I simply adhered to the crucial medical instructions (in which I was not proficient) until the medics arrived. Other than being wet, shocked and astonished, it ended up being all good; once again with God's grace and empowerment of courage, I helped the Mrs. change her clothes and hours later, returned to my home whereupon I took a nice, long, rejuvenating shower.

Having to report my daily results every night (via voicemail) to my office, as I tried to leave my required, detailed phone message, I found myself in tears over this astonishing event. I had contact with the Mrs. and her caregiver subsequently as I had to visit them in the hospital. During this unfortunate episode, I'll never forget the sticky situation that occurred while trying to revive this aged gentleman while I was still at his home. The wife had urgently instructed me to call their son who lived nearby and so I did. As I juggled communicating with the medics, the son arrived. The son ultimately found out why I was there, and as his dad lay on his deathbed being lifted into the ambulance, the son confronted me trying to corner me, all while I was getting into my car. He began asking questions as to "who was getting what" through their wills, etc, and, once again, I stood up like a peacock and slammed him into shame. I wasn't being judgmental. I was being factual. That is "NO" as I say to pets... animals need to be trained. It never ceases to amaze me how many family members so selfishly want to know what they are "getting" before their loved ones even pass. Seriously, go find your own $75.

The faith you place unto and into God, family, and friends will come back to you in multitudes. Keep your head high and you will always find the strength and courage to be the person God has intended you to be. Stay alert, sharp, open-minded and not opinionated and continue enhancing your skills and abilities. Be cognizant of the deceitful backstabbers who hug and smile at you daily and perhaps take you to a $75 lunch. At the same time... who has time for that, right? When something falls or fails, try to refrain from making indecisive quick-fix decisions. Take a step back for a few minutes away from the situation you're frustrated with, take a deep breath and take another look at it after reevaluating. Know who your peeps are, your mentors and resources and establish your common denominators. Stick with your own program, that which has historically worked for you. You may need to make a few tweaks, but just keep it real and simple. It truly pays to have a beautiful realm of marvelous friendships and not merely acquaintances.

ADVENTURES AT WALMART

Tracy and I ventured to Walmart recently. I love me some Wally World, but sometimes the adventures are a little too crowded for me (and most anyone else) who especially patrons the store on weekends. But in this instance, it was thankfully, in the morning on a weekday. After the completion of our shopping spree, we were to meet at the cash register after we each shopped on opposite sides of the store. Being the frugal person I am and upon heading to the checkout line, I wondered where her Gemini multi-tasking self was. I passed by the rotisserie chickens. Ummm. God forbid we analyze grocery items and prices when we're hungry- you'll spend an extra $75 because when you're hungry you don't give a rat's ass how much something costs while you're shopping. Everything becomes a bargain... and the fact that I love chicken and eat it nearly every day was a factor. Never go shopping when you're hungry, right? Well after the aroma hit my stomach I eyeballed the price and thought "really, only $2.44"? It doesn't look rotten, so I merrily slid it into my cart after practically analyzing the skin off of it.   I then got in line, still trying to figure out why it was so cheap. About that time, Tracy had found me in line. Her and her sarcasm...being that she had worked for Walmart long ago. She cracked up at my cheap chicken resting in my cart and said to me- "you Goober head – 2:44 is the time they placed the chicken out here...not the price of it." Whatever. I'm not the chicken police and that detail was not clear-- not to me, anyway. I grilled my chicken and ate it right away, although I knew something was up with that price—there just was simply no "semi-colon" on the label. It was a "period" instead.

CHANGE IS GOOD

Make an investment in yourself by putting as much time and energy into yourself as you do with others. Be prideful and joyful with and to yourself as you do with others and make sure you check your mirror daily. Combine your positive energies and experiences and MAKE THAT DIFFERENCE even if it means change; most folks are so afraid of change. Change can be good. Change is ALL good sometimes-take a chance-keep faith in yourself. Take a leap of faith if you have to and be proud and confident. Rest comfortably on that pillow every night. Keep it real and simple, knowing that it will all be good, through God.

Yesterday I was 5. When I woke up this morning I was 90. We're never promised tomorrow because it is what it is at the present and time essentially flies by us like a freight train. We can only do so much with what we have set forth in front of us. We must be mindful to be logical and frugal and learn how to handle what is on our plate at the given moment. When you truly focus on your plate and not that of others, you'll have more time and stamina to sustain a healthier and more developed, confident attitude.

Sometimes during an estate planning consultation, I have to calmly reassure folks in a hugging, matter-of-fact, velvet-hammer kind of way to be mindful too, that when you are forecasting your demise, there is the fact of WHEN we die, not IF we die. I don't use scare tactics with folks, just reality and certainty.

Keeping things real and simple has helped me not only in my professional development, but also in my personal development. For instance- when calling a company such as our utility bill creditors, I hope (sometimes to no avail) to talk with a live representative and try to avoid the phone automation- seriously? It has gotten to be so cumbersome and frustrating these day, has it not? Where has the simplicity gone? I'm not calling God here. I can't afford that expensive international phone rate. I have His number on another plan any way. In any event, we must acknowledge that we are not in the old school any more when it comes to these phone systems being automated. Keep it real and simple. Usually, by simply pressing the number "0" several times during these aggravating calls (feeling like we are being bounced around the phone galaxy) and then pressing the applicable number to either discontinue service, pay a bill or acquire some kind of stock in the company if you may- a live representative will answer the phone. Automation can stink- and furthermore- this virtual worldly voice has the audacity to ask us initially to # (pound) over to select one of the 5 languages they don't even speak! How about listening to my initial verbal request, Mr. and/or Mrs. Virtual, and interpret it your Clampett-self for the $75 I pay you folks every month! I'm just saying...you'll find there are so many people and companies who never get the mere fact that simple is simple. Period. Mr. and Mrs. Drama need to be introduced to simplicity in my opinion. That's another chapter in itself. Again, I'm just saying... just by keeping things real and simple, you can make yourself and others pleasantly happy. Simply happy.

Remember the simple and fundamental things in life, that the sun (SON) is always shining but we simply can't always see it. Refrain from burning bridges and crying over spilled milk. Again, remember that the hand we may shake one day going up the corporate ladder or the like, may be the same hand we shake one day while going back down that same ladder. I've seen that happen to many folks who've straddled a high horse. Whether it be professional or family-oriented, it could be a harsh fall if you don't encompass yourself with humbleness.

REMEMBERING TERRY

My sister Terry and her boyfriend had visited me from WV one weekend before we headed out together to do our traditional "family" visitation with our folks at Christmas. She was so excited, as always, about reuniting with the family (which was usually only once a year). Her excitement and joy was so spirited, full of love and compassion and humor- always tapping her foot while enjoying our family's spirit fill the air in fellowship, music and gratitude. Sometimes it was a mere circular, family chitchat filled with warmth and laughter, and sometimes it was us playing music as if the Mandrel sisters were in the house, dueling our voices and musical instruments together in such sweet harmony. Not only was she an awesome person, but an incredible pianist and vocalist. Terry actually was in a high school play with the famous and talented, Grammy award-winning recording artist, Kathy Mattea. In her spare time Terry played on an international pool league and frequently went to Vegas on tournaments, where she had a jovial blast. I have her beautiful monogrammed, championship jackets that keep me and my family smiling, embracing her achievements. She worked for the largest law firm in her state, back in the day, and her colleagues were all just as sweetly spirited as she was, especially throughout the funeral process, extending every considerate yet sorrowful measure to ascertain our peace and comfort on behalf of their firm. God bless them for their spirit and sincere sorrow and kindness. They had an incredible, populated, tribute to her when we went to the first funeral in WV. Many spirited people were there expressing such love and compassion, in some sort of blissful sorrow. The overwhelming moment was somewhat blurred for me at that immediate time but soon after became more vivid once I started to tango with Mr. Resilient. He was extremely challenging to waltz with, per say, and later gave me the most fragrant rose I'd ever smelled.

After the spokesperson expressed many beautiful words during the tribute, they unexpectedly and so graciously unveiled a very large, vibrant and gorgeous painting of Terry. The firm had hired an artist to compose this painting to reflect Terry's life- depicting her wholesome dedication to the entire law firm, to her family, to friends and to her loving community. They expressed an appreciation of her loyalty, dedication, spirit and personality. It was a large, colorful painting which brought forth Terry's life, her character, her personality, and talents; gifts that she had blessed the

71

world with when she was here. The portrait was dedicated to her by her law firm "in loving memory to their beloved friend and colleague." It was an amazing, spirited and inspirational moment and memorial. The portrait is gorgeous and so accurately portrayed her beautiful legacy. The top of the painting portrays a very nice t-shirt and baseball glove with the law firm's logo. Terry really rocked at softball and had fun with it as with everything else she encountered. Next was a tightly racked set of billiard balls depicting her exciting moments of glory with her team of pool league champions. Then there is a beautiful bald eagle reflecting that she headed up an Eagles Auxiliary Club. There was also the iconic emblem of The American Red Cross where she so proudly managed blood drives in the community for many years. Continuing on was a favorite of mine, a beautiful guitar gently resting against the side of a gorgeous piano. I frequently played the guitar with her and Karen, singing in 3- part harmony with Mom and Dad being the backup "Pips." The next part of the portrait portrays a bowling ball (she had also been in a successful bowling league), then some colorful trees of the forest, which are indicative of how she marveled camping, wildlife and nature itself. Years ago, I recall that Terry and some of her friends were being chased by a black bear while on a camping trip. They were driving in a truck and she was in the bed of the truck praying for them to "mash the gas" I'm sure. I can just picture her trying to talk some sense into the bear to scare him away. She was a hoot! The last part of the painting is a beautiful, blooming red rose which simply represented her spirit and the fact that the law firm always sent their employees a red rose on their birthday.

All of this beauty was simply painted and surrounded by the constant streams of the Kanawha River which flowed through her town and by the sidewalk where she walked for many, many years, simply enjoying and appreciating life. She loved boating, the water and the regattas, and used to always say "you gotta regatta"! Believe you me, I know she's still doing her regatta because It's All Good, especially with the pennies she has sent me.

I would always take a menu request from Terry over the phone prior to her coming to visit because she so loved cooking out on the grill, peacefully enjoying the flickering tiki-torches and tropical palm plants that surrounded my patio, giving a comfortable setting. Of course I would always cook her favorite; shrimp, chicken and beef kabobs with onions, peppers, mushrooms, tomatoes and pineapple, all marinated with a combo of pineapple juice, butter and teriyaki sauce. It's yummy. While grilling she would occasionally come into the house and hide one of the Ficus trees from my den. I'd act like I wouldn't notice and then I'd take it from where she had hidden it and hide it somewhere else. One day it even ended up outside in my neighbor's yard. I'd quickly go and retrieve it as I cried laughing at her foolishness. She was quite fun, funny, smart and had such a joyful soul. Funny thing is that she still is a blast- throwing those darn pennies at my freakin' shoes. How about throwing me some Clampett-kabobs, girlfriend? I'd give her $75 for a plate of them right about now! I always feel her spirit when I remember her smiling at me, overhearing me in my office telling me that I'm really good at what I do. No Sis, you are awesome at what you've done and what you're still doing now. As a matter of fact, after having that long, spirited phone conversation with my mother over coffee, as she verbally outlined the details of the aforementioned portrait, I felt a great sense of awe, and decided to go play the piano for a moment. Notably, I indeed had a lot of polishing up to do after many years of long gaps in not tickling the ivory. I wasn't certain what to play (that I had remembered to play "by ear"), but as soon as I sat down on the piano bench-without hesitation- I felt inspired and began playing "How Great Thou Art." I had never played that song on the piano before and furthermore I didn't have a sheet of music in front of me either. I somehow played the beautiful song flawlessly, as if I'd been playing it for years and years. There were other listeners lingering and admiring the music, apparently, and I was practically drained and limp afterwards as if my energy had been silently exhausted. Suffice it to say, it was an incredibly overwhelming sensation and a warm, wonderful feeling came over me. T'was quite symbolic that it was indeed all good and that "It's All Good."

So many friends have come into my humble abode and glanced at some of my framed photographs of family and friends. The photos and the friends, albeit. One is a gorgeous picture of my sister, Karen, who got married to a marvelous man about two years ago. It was the most gorgeous wedding I'd ever attended, and I'd never been so excited and proud of her, and for her. Like Terry, she's very highly regarded and respected by her family, friends and colleagues, and is so very beautiful in spirit, mind and body; always a hit in my household with respect to her beautiful photos that I display; and always "my rock, my sister," the One who really "knows" me as well as "sees" me, just as I do her.

My photos are worth millions to me. Their presence offers me so much comfort and joy, as if the arms of my family embrace me. Whether its a good day or a bad day, I feel the presence of my family and their love. My sweet, sweet Terry, although you have left me in this lifetime, I know that you are with me in spirit, all of the time. Rest in peace dear sister and always know how much I love you.

JETTA ROW THE BOAT ASHORE

Karen had a black lab many years ago named Jetta, who happened to be my only niece, and she loved her Auntie Vicki as much as I loved her. She was a loving, loyal, beautiful master-oriented dog and endlessly loved my Sis, her "Mama." One day, many moons ago, as my sister was planning her upcoming wedding, she requested that I play my trumpet in her wedding. My sister that is, not Jetta. I honestly cringe when I have to speak or perform in front of folks but she knew I'd go to the moon and back for her, just as she would for me. Knowing how her wedding was so beautifully and mindfully planned and orchestrated with such a personal, intimate touch and thought-out venue, it was a very exciting time, despite how my stomach churned with stage fright. Because the wedding was to take place at a quaint outdoor chapel, I felt inclined to find my personal comfort level in practicing there because I hadn't played my trumpet outdoors since I was in the marching band in high school. It was a beautiful, sunny day in October when she and I and Jetta went to this outdoor chapel in an attempt to have a little fun in the sun, relax and perhaps get out on the water, that is after I practiced playing melodic harmonies into the wilderness and into the falling leaves. The quaint chapel was located alongside a small lake, privately owned, I'm sure, and had a rowboat nestled along the dock. Before we pleasured ourselves with having fun in the sun, I practiced the Lord's Prayer on my trumpet as Sis peacefully laid on the concrete bench surrounded by large stones and beautiful forestry and colorful leaves. It was evident that she was indulging her mind and body into the sounds of the falling leaves that would perhaps cushion her tomorrows and the spirit of God and the sanctity of unity.

Shortly after practicing, we strolled down the pier to find the sturdy little rowboat which had Jetta's name and my name written all over it. I looked down at Jetta with excitement and promptly found a daunting stick to toss. She peripherally saw my glares of challenge and knew the game was on. I threw the large stick out as far as I could to the center of the small lake. As I quickly rustled into the rowboat I saw her muscular oars starting to row as strongly as mine. Mine were wooden mind you. Every few seconds she would glance over at me (not back at me albeit) with her piercing eyes and saw my excited, eager ambition. The closer we got to the stick, the more we stretched our necks out to victory, the more tickled I became and I ultimately just simply let her win. Actually, my rowboat toppled over my rubber-necking Clampett-self and the bubbles of laughter roared from underneath my liquid torture as I tried to surface for air. If the water and been warmer I would have been okay. But it was quite cold and scary-until I heard my sister running along the perimeter of the shoreline-laughing hysterically. Believe me, I was laughing so hard with her because I could only imagine what a scene this had been. Jetta strenuously helped pull me out from a deep embankment on that cold, yet fun and exciting day. Precious memories with a treasured sister and niece are incredible and immeasurable and shall be treasured forever.

I'M JUST SAYIN'

With respect to BFFs, be alert and mindful of who's coming and going in your life, i.e. the Mr. and Mrs. Important who's world is always the only world that exists. Short-term friends can be an exhausting encounter. "Qualify" your friends with the understanding of who your common-denominator types of friends truly are. Don't let Mr. and Mrs. Important forcefully throw "bowling balls" at you expecting miracles and leaving and re-entering your life. Establish your boundaries with your friends and/or colleagues and make wise decisions when selecting folks to actually be your friend in lieu of mere acquaintances. Sometimes when you make time to take a couple of steps back and reevaluate things in a different perspective, you'll find the importance in making yourself happy instead of trying to accommodate someone else's expectations of you. Once again, life is about you too, not just others all of the time. It's about making yourself happy with a thick security blanket of boundaries around your plate of life. Most of us would rather have a few outstanding warm friends who truly appreciate and respect us rather than a zillion acquaintances that will ultimately exhaust us. Keep things real and simple, and it will all be good.

Turn your television off sometimes and listen to some tunes to get away from the world. Appreciate those who you grew up with; Michael J., Whitney H., etc. Share a moment with them and mindfully let them know that you appreciate the way they shared their spirit through their music while they walked the earth. Simply smile and open a door for someone...sometimes that's a musical gesture in itself.

Let folks know that you appreciate them before it's "too late." Again, we are never promised tomorrow and should truly not take things for granted- the simplicity of our running water, each other, conveniences, or life itself. We can drown in greed and self-absorption which may ultimately be destructive. Don't lose consciousness of what is laid before us and learn to appreciate and respect what you have, and who you are.

During weak moments and delicate situations, try to find the strength to pull the bull by the horns and take charge of those pertinent matters that are in your control. Have a strong understanding from within that you are indeed a strong person- that you are blessed and count your blessings. Let your inspired spirit shine from the reflection of your heart and soul. Many smiles result from such simple gestures. I've learned many things through many different situations-not necessarily mine, but those of others, that sometimes people and things get misconstrued or misunderstood. Some folks are intimidated or jealous of others but it is what it is. All individuals have their own idiosyncrasies. Keep it real and simple and charge anyone a fat $75 for their inaccurate assumptions of you, if applicable. Live, learn, and love and be proud of who you are- once again, do a mirror check and hug yourself daily knowing God is truly in control and that you are simply trying to be the best person you can be. I'm just sayin...

Get to know yourself again and set your boundaries in life, keeping things real and simple. Focus on yourself in lieu of spending a large percent of your time focusing on someone else. Take things in stride and know your limitations, taking precautions with pride and confidence. Keep with "the program" and keep your head out of the sand. Some of those crabs have sharp claws.

It's healthy to focus on your contentment and prosperity. Once again, it's your pillow that you must sleep on at night, and it's the one and only mirror you have to face every day. Keep mindful to "judge not that ye be not judged." We all do it. Keep it real and simple.

In dealing with many folks over the years, laughingly, I've heard so many stories get so twisted. People get so wrapped up in gossip and such- simply tend to your own plate- it's so much easier. Many folks, once again, tend to get intimidated by others who are simply trying to achieve their own success story; but sometimes they unfortunately get things twisted.

Just because someone is confident, self-assured, loved, loving and strong doesn't mean that they are cocky or better than others... and it doesn't mean that it makes the other person bigger when they try to bring you down and make you feel inadequate. That's their plate to deal with. Those folks should perhaps try to find themselves and find their God and refrain from looking down their long nose at others. There are a lot of folks out there like that unfortunately, from what I've noticed. I'm not being judgmental here, only factual. Find peace with or within yourself and it will help console any insecurity you may have.

After Terry's death, my soul was nearly exhausted and my energies depleted. I am so truly blessed to have had the strong family and friends that held each other's hands and consoled each others hearts throughout that tragedy. I recall strolling down my driveway one afternoon, and being the "rose sniffer" that I am, I actually SAW a rose. I leaned over the fragrant, thorny shrub and actually "smelled" once again. I "felt" once again. It was nice to feel the sensation of a pleasant aroma and have a velvety visual to accompany it. Smiling, I chuckled and thought, it's all good, finally. And it's all God. It sure as heck wasn't me who was a strong peacock leading into this pivotal moment with my weakened self! It takes a long minute to get your senses back, or your life for that matter, but it is what it is. AND IT WAS WHAT IT WAS. The power of prayer, strength and faith is beyond rewarding. Just remember who's got your steering wheel. With faith and gratitude you just merely have to let loose of your tight grip on the steering wheel. With endurance and strength, we will find that God doesn't put more on our plate than we can handle. Ultimately, we may find it's simply a puppy in the center of our plate that needs to be nurtured, and not the drama of the world. Keep it real. Keep it simple. Don't be blinded by the trees from the forest. It's all good, through the graciousness of God.

AGAIN, I'M JUST SAYIN'

It's important to know who your resources are on this earth. Know who to contact when you need an electrician, a plumber, or insurance agent; know your neighbors and church members if applicable. Knowing who your contact people are in an immediate situation will help anchor your well-being. Get organized with your own personal resources by simply being your own personal resource within yourself.

Sometimes we take problems or situations out of element or context and in trying to make our own resolutions or answers we find that it might not be the one that God is simply placing in front of us. Be open- minded and flexible in trying to find, embrace and reason what your purpose in life may be. Take your cues in your journey of life, whether it be pursuing a career in music, raising a large family, or milking cows on a dairy farm. Take pride in the value you bring to the precious plate of life. Yesterday I was 5 and when I woke up this morning I was 90. Know that whatever doesn't kill you just simply makes you stronger. Again, remember that the sun is always out but we just simply can't always see it. Find the fun in creating objects or animals out of the clouds above. Find the strength in yourself and through God, and stand tall however short you are, and be strong and diligent. Keep your faith, the faith in yourself, and stay polished in your everyday pursuits and know that your $75 will be in the mail at some point and time, in some fashion, shape or form. Seriously.

I've always felt that if we can do things in moderation, not always defined by Webster's Dictionary, things can typically be all good and kosher. But when someone, for instance, sits in front of you with a plate full of stacked donuts (which a friend of mine recently did) and questions why they are so heavy- not the donuts- it's hard to be polite and honestly discreet in your reply. Sometimes less is more. Again, not necessarily the donuts. Sometimes more donuts feels like a stress reliever to us. It's hard not to suggest that someone push back from the table, especially if you know you need to be pushing back from it as well...Fatty, fatty, two by four... The intoxicating love of sweets is a battlefield. I gain 5 pounds just thinking of the word chocolate, or bacon, or food period. Heck, I could lick the residue from a packet of sweet-n-low and my eyelashes will stand on end. Bottom line here is that the less enticement you have from anything adverse around you makes it less tempting to indulge. But you'll eventually realize you've reached your bar of combat when you feel that your game is on. It's fun to swing from the trees sometimes when we know where they are and how to swing fluently among the shadows through them.

I'd recently been dog-sitting for 2 weeks for my friends who traveled to Canada. They had entrusted me with their aging dog (a huge Pug) who is diabetic and requires lots of love and attention- and insulin shots twice daily. Having to physically "carry" him up and down my steps several times a day just to do his business, I simply realized that it was merely a nice "workout" for me (in addition to him) to get some exercise and enjoy my long-term canine friend. One morning as I awoke from my couch which I'd rested upon overnight, I heard him whimpering and I quickly arose to let him out. One of his beds I'd stationed him upon lay beside my sofa- my entire house was his bed, actually. I quickly noticed that he wasn't at the door as I heard his whimpers and I couldn't quite tell where he actually was. After calling his name, he kept whining and I was perplexed because I could tell he was nearby and was probably in some sort of dire sugary straits. And I don't mean insulin. I became somewhat amused because I knew that a granule of hidden food or a lodged toy was involved somewhere in the vicinity. As I glanced over at the love-seat, all I could see was his fat white cellulite ass sticking straight up in the air-stuck straight up towards the moon. Bless his heart. All because of a strayed, stale potato chip. Even dogs have their weaknesses.

THE LOOK OF DEATH

My sister Karen is one of the most beautiful, bright, intelligent, comedic and fun-spirited people I've ever known and will always be cherished. Neither of us are professionals at snow-skiing, however, she does a great job at water skiing. That was our forte. Certainly, she has stories of her own to share about Ms. Clampett, herself I'm sure. We grew up very close-knit and were disciplined like some folks in DC should be. Again, just being factual here, not judgmental. We grew up playing sports, water skiing, bowling, tennis, sledding and tubing down snowy mountainsides; played racquetball, and sang in the church choir. Mom would pinch the heck out of us in church when we started giggling. I could hardly ever sit beside sis, especially in the choir pit. I almost had to exit from singing in the choir one afternoon because of her spontaneous wit. She's quite hilarious. And quite a faithful icon that any family tree should be proudly imprinted with.

One beautiful, snowy weekend we packed up and headed to the snowy, white-capped mountains of NC to go snow skiing. We love the snow and have built many snowmen together in our younger days and made snow cream, which is awesome-of course you have to wait until the 2nd snow to make your snow cream to ascertain that it's edible and of course you never want to make it if the snow is polluted or yellow by any means. We were so excited to go snow skiing together. It was a given that we'd have an exciting, competitive blast together and enjoy the awesome, fun friends we were with.

We eventually settled in our gorgeous lodge and powdery surroundings and acquired our ski passes and such for the next day. As morning approached and after spending an endless amount of time putting on our 1000 pounds of clothes, boots and skis, I thought, SERIOUSLY...? We do this "why"? Way too much armor to be strapping on... This was either my first or second time snow skiing and I knew very quickly that we were in for an interesting ride. One of us would soon be busting our tails-either laughing or crying. I wondered, who would it be?

In a hilarious effort to simply make it to the bunny slopes, I remember feeling like a tarantula just trying to get my Clampett-self there, laughing our tails off at each other the whole way. The lodge is located near beautiful Asheville, NC which is a "must-see" city- a gorgeous place to visit. After practicing a while, we advanced to the intermediate slope watching the folks become tiny as we advanced up the intimidating, majestic mountain. As she and I rode together up the ski lift, we agreed to meet somewhere down below just simply "whenever" or "however" in my case. Being competitive sisters, we were just simply having fun. I lost track of her after being shuffled down the slope from the chair lift and prayed that I wouldn't embarrass myself or her, nor kill anyone in the process. Trying my best to swerve from left to right so as not to gain too much speed, and ski like you're supposed too, I found myself accelerating much more than I anticipated. I was TOTALLY out of control and scared to pieces. I briefly saw her in my right peripheral and witnessed her astonishment. I recall her tense glare as if she quickly noticed I had the fear of God in my face. Of course she was laughing her tail off at me and as I flew by her; I could feel her fingers crossing for me. In advance and just in case, I began apologizing to whomever it be that I might plow down at the end of the slope. Whew, what a ride.

REELLY, POP?

Speaking of skiing and being competitive in our younger day, Mom and Pop frequently took us boating and camping. We have been so very blessed to have had that warm family time as we do today. As a youngster, Pop would get me up early in the morning (like 4 o'clock) to go fishing with him (which we all so loved to do) and I would do so under 2 conditions. Number one is that he would bait the nasty worm on my hook when I ran out of crickets, and number two is that he would take me water skiing in the afternoon until I was pooped and dropped. I despised getting up early and I still do. That was when I started setting the bar high. Most of the time we came to a mutual agreement with our negotiating skills, especially when I always promised not to tell Mom or anyone else that I'd caught more fish than he did. It was the least of his fisherman's stories...Furthermore, the tiny fish he'd reel in were the size of my hand, not his- and vice versa. He could never keep those reeling stories real. Getting back home where Mom awaited the catch of the day (the fish, not my Dad) was so much fun. We'd always have a scrumptious fish fry that evening as we relaxed and watched our freckles connect, hence acquiring a nice tan from so much fun in the sun.

Over the years, Dad effortlessly mastered pulling a skier behind the boat and above the heavy layers of water, while scouting and navigating the calmest of coves, by keeping things real and simple. He knew how to "drop off" the tired skier when they signaled they were ready to let go of the rope at their destination. Before I learned how to slalom, I skied on two skis as did my sister but I enjoyed the slalom more. Less was more even back then. Many times, Karen and I would ski together from behind our small boat -so proudly and with so much united charisma- as if we were on tour as part of the Cypress Garden Water-skiing Gals. Aside from pretending to be so Clampett-glamorous on skis, we'd exchange a few jolting humorous attempts to make each other fall. She would do things with her skis that are even haunting to remember.

How challenging that truly is while you're holding onto a rope! If it could be done, we did it. However, comfortably sitting on the back of a boat as a spectator, while facing the skier making faces and gestures, and trying to distract them into losing their balance and falling is so much simpler. It would have really been funny if one of us had "flashed" the skier (when no one was looking of course) to try and make them fall into the water and lose their skis. I'm not saying that I ever did that type of nonsense or anything...

One exciting, sunny afternoon at Dad's company picnic, while skiing, Pop had simply "dropped me off" at our sandy destination and as my ski hit the sand I simply stepped out from it and went and sat down to relax with a soda. Later that day, I was admiring my beautiful sister doing the same thing, skiing so gracefully. However, when she eventually let go of the rope and sailed to the sandy shore, her skis crushed into the sand and in the matter of a split second, she ended up face down in the sand. I mean nose down, head, face...(twas funny then). It just happened so quick. In these situations you pray they're okay and not laugh out loud so that anyone can hear. It was quite funny, bless her heart. She was fine of course, except for her pride. We've all seen each other fall many times and not necessarily always on a sandy shore. Some falls are harder and some are perhaps funnier than others. Remember that laughter is the best medicine and we've all got to embrace that fact.

We were both at our parent's church a few years ago and were sitting in the balcony admiring the beautiful "Living Christmas Tree" being performed by the beautiful and talented church members. They sounded so angelic. My parents were sitting behind us. I knew not to look at my sister during the sermon because she always cracks me up, especially in church, and she says a lot without merely saying a word at all. Well, she said a word and I sat there for 30 minutes I know, cupping my mouth and closing my eyes feeling makeup running down my face. I know my parents saw our shoulders shaking. You can dress us up but you just can't be sure what will happen if you take us out together, I reckon. A few years prior we were once again at their church attending a function with their beautiful Sunday School Class. That day my eyes were extremely watery due to allergies and I had to constantly wipe the tears from around my eyes. My sister leaned over and grabbed my hand and uttered something to the effect that it was okay to repent and that everything will be okay. I told her she had to stop, people were staring. Mom and Dad should have known that even as adults, we still shouldn't attend church together. My sister. My BFF. Priceless.

IT'S "POSTON" BUTT SPELLED LIKE "BOSTON"

Speaking of BFFs, Mom is the best cook in the world... my beautiful Aunt Nora Lee taught her well... and vice-versa. One of our all-time favorites that Mom prepares especially at Christmas, is called "grits and ham liquor." You simply cook the grits in the ham broth (liquor as it's called) that you had cooked the ham or Boston Butt in (that's a piece of meat you know.) It's so savory and such a staple here in the south. My Dad would get so upset if you even thought about throwing away any leftover grits. And he meant that fact! One day at a family outing at their home, located in the deep south, and after scarfing down what felt like a pound of grits and eggs, my dad was peacefully relaxing on the back deck with a cup of coffee, watching the colorful chirping birds and listening to us girls giggling the whole time we were cleaning the kitchen. Karen and I would snarl and grunt and sigh at each other as if the other wasn't pulling her weight in getting the kitchen cleaned up. We were jokingly giving each other nasty looks and whispering hateful, snide remarks to each other, just being hilariously venomous while crying and laughing at our warped sense of humor. Having had to outwit each other was perhaps a simple exchange of $75. Mom had "our number" as she just chuckled in the background- probably wondering where the stork unfortunately got misdirected in route (or should I say root) many moons ago.

We had a lot of leftover grits that morning since Mom always "positioned" herself during her preparation to have plenty of leftover grits for Pop. With that said, I plotted something humorous to "get his goat" as we say in the south-but in essence, it was meant to ruffle his fluffy feathers. After emptying the leftover grits into a Tupperware bowl and placing them in the fridge, I took the empty pot of "air" grits and held it like a drum in my arms with a big spoon dangling in my hand and darted out of the house and across the lawn, marching toward the woods for "the scraping." Noticing Pop watching me from my peripheral, I was nonchalant and kept my head lowered so he wouldn't see me on the edge of cracking up. I could feel his intense stare in wonderment and knew he was going to start getting fidgety, rubbing his fingers together and start to boil and become humorously dramatic. And he did... Bless his heart. As I heard him begin to clear his throat, and as I landed toe to toe with the edge of the woods, I started scraping the already emptied-out pot as loudly as I could and he bolted out of his chair screaming for the salvation of his grits. You would have thought someone had shot him! Laughingly, I eventually gave in and assured him that I was just messing with him and that his grits, all 12,564 of them were safely being preserved in the fridge. He'd cut my tail if I had tossed those grits. My friends who come to visit my family fall in love with Mom's grits. And my family. Tracy loves them (in this case, the grits) so much that she stood up from the table after enjoying the savory grits and commented that she just wanted to slap everybody! An ole southern saying after a good eatin' is "it just makes me wanna slap ya mamma"!

IT IS!   IT IS SNOWING!

Many years ago, and I mean many, my parents had decided to relocate back up to the Carolina's from having resided in the southern depths of Georgia. We were all so tickled pink to have them transfer back closer to home. With having made that move, Karen no longer had the opportunity to read the zillion mile markers to me during our long trips to visit them and additionally we wouldn't spit on each other as a result of it. Because their decision was made at Christmas time, we simply had to overcome the challenge of where the Christmas festivities would take place...somewhere and somewhat accommodating and geographically conducive to all of our living situations. As Mom and Dad transitioned, they temporarily resided in a small house (which was too small for the given celebration) until the sale of their newly acquired home eventually finalized. Terry and Karen were living too far north for it to be a convenient center point, and I was ironically residing in the center of all of the options, in a Clampett small house, needless to say, (thank goodness)! At the time it wasn't Clampett, but it was too small to accommodate everyone. After exchanging simple thoughts, we agreed to station our Christmas celebration at a very gorgeous venue- "over the river and through the woods"- underneath the heavy pines at a very lovely and private condo resort located at beautiful Lake Lure, NC where our folks had a timeshare and which rectified the accommodating needs for all of us. It was so exciting being in the mountains again, especially at Christmas time, with the family, including our God-Parents, Aunt Lucy and Uncle Zeke. And I brought my can of fake snow I'd spontaneously placed in my travel bag while packing. I wasn't certain as to if or how I'd use it, but I knew it would not stay full for very long.

Having previously lived in the beautiful mountains of WV as a youngster, Mom and I always shared at least one passionate thing in common: the love of snow. The anticipation of it's arrival, watching the delicate flakes fall before they landed, building very friendly snowmen, having competitive snowball fights, and plucking icicles hanging tightly from the sides of the mountains are such precious memories. But the mere anticipation of the snowfall was the greatest excitement of it all. During this Christmas vacation, Mom and I stayed finely tuned in, and I mean adamantly, to the weather forecast for snow, and we knew it was well on its way. We could just smell it in the air! And what's Christmas without snow anyway? We just knew that God would make it all good.

Our comfortable condo sat underneath some beautiful sagging pines where the melting snow had lingered. The sliding glass doors that surrounded our comfort zone enabled us to relax inside of our cozy quarters while savoring the intake of Mother Nature in Her entirety. The squirrels were so playful and cute; and plump- Lil' fatties they were- they would literally have playful dances- or prayer meetings on the deck it seemed, while they scrambled around for more nuts- as if we hadn't constantly been placing nuts out in bowls for them for their own little furry Christmas party. They would glare at us through the sliding glass doors for long periods at a time, as if "we" were the ones who were actually "sliding" (not the doors) and not constantly feeding them all the nuts their tiny little hearts desired. Little did they know that we were actually the biggest nuts they were gleaming at inside through the thick door, and they'd better watch their pesky little attitudes because I noticed there were some mighty big pots nestled up in the kitchen! I'll show them how to throw acorns!

Mom had been in the kitchen passionately cooking and joyfully listening to us all-not missing a word of what we were saying or a beat as to what Johnny Mathis was singing. She was enjoying being alone in the kitchen as we all do sometimes, but in this case was totally enjoying dancing with Mr. Mathis and his festive Christmas tunes on her dance floor. What a sight. He could simply cry you into believing in Santa Clause if, by chance, Virginia, you didn't.

Well, the weather outside was frightful, and the fire was so delightful...turn the lights down on low, and let it snow, let it snow, (and so I went to go get my can of it,) let it snow! I just knew I was once again going straight to jail and not collecting $200. We all knew that the area had an ongoing, exciting forecast of snow...so with that in mind, I slid to my bedroom and snatched my can of snow from my bag and nonchalantly strolled through the living room with my finger pressed to my lips, quietly asking everyone to "roll with me" on this one for a few minutes. All I could see was their teeth through their muffled laughs noticing the can of snow in my hand as I quietly marched out onto the deck into the "silent night" of what was soon to become a stroll of "walking in the winter wonderland."

The floodlights "and stars were brightly shining," and so I stood flush against the outside wall of the condo underneath the floodlights, trying to stay hidden and not be seen through the doors from the inside. Holding the can in the air, I started spraying the snow at an angle from underneath the lighting and quickly peeked through the glass to witness a quick thumbs up. Moments after this sudden snowfall, excitement began to fill the air on the inside as I heard everyone exclaim, " It's snowing! It's snowing! It is! It is snowing"! they chanted. All of a sudden, the only thing I could hear was the pitter-patter of the vibrating steps of Mom abruptly dashing away from her dance partner in the kitchen, galloping through the condo toward the wintry wonderland and onto the dance floor of the snowy deck. The way she jolted that heavy sliding glass door open, you would have thought she stood more than a mere five feet tall. I felt that David was once again about to face Goliath. As she approached the deck, not noticing me whatsoever flushed into the darkness, she raised her hands high into the air and with all of her excitement shouted "It's snowing! It is snowing"! She was doing a happy dance! Everyone was doing a happy dance! It was snowing! And I was about to pee all over myself. As she heard me nearly explode and eventually turned around, I thought "go ahead and handcuff me." Instead she repeatedly beat the pure mess out of me with a stack of very heavy duty paper plates she'd had in her hands all this time. I understand that was an ugly thing to have done, but it was indeed many, many years ago that I pulled that prank... with the support of my fearless, encouraging posse who still gets choked up when re-living that memory. Although Mom also felt the great sense of humor in it all, let it be known that Karma has had many deserving prayer meetings with me since then.

PAPER OR PLASTIC, MAM?

One of my "common-denominator friends", LB, is also a colleague of mine and has been for many years. She's bright and overall beautiful. And although she is very professional, she is quite hilarious-especially when you don't expect it. Having known each other for many years, she called me one day and asked if I would play a prank on her mom. SERIOUSLY?

Her mom lives a few houses down from her and they are very close-knit, having contact with each other several times a day. That said, LB explained to me that her mom's neighbor who lived behind her (the mom) had some chickens that kept getting loose in her backyard causing chaotic mayhem in her manicured lawn and pine straw in her flower beds. Her mom, "Bunny Smith" we'll say, and I have never met personally, but we've talked many times on the phone over the years and have always somewhat felt like family- in my mind's eye. She's a great person to know and converse with-bright, vibrant and warm-spirited, just like LB.

After taking a few minutes to work up a hand-written plan for the prank, I called LB and advised her to conduct a 3-way call and get her mom on the phone. I also told LB to mute her phone because I knew she would eventually make me crack up. Yet another prank, I thought. Here goes another 3-way with me, God, and Satan himself. Not! Just an analogy. God would always win because "it's all good."

Here's how it all went down after several rings:

> "Ms. Smith"? I asked as she answered the phone.
>
> "Yes"? She replied.
>
> "Ms. Bunny L. Smith"?
>
> "Yes"? She said smilingly.
>
> Hello. This is Carol Stevens with the Union County Animal control Center; how are YOU today''?
>
> "Oh, hello Ms. Stevens" she said.

I could just feel LB cracking up through the muted phone. It was quite difficult to maintain my composure as the conversation got deeper and deeper with respects to the loose chickens and the mayhem they'd been causing. I told her that we'd been notified by a few of her neighbors, that her chickens were viciously tearing up their yards, and that we had animal control officers in pursuit to capture the chickens to remedy the destructive nonsense. She was so alarmingly surprised but yet became quite compassionate, eventually asking that we don't hurt her chickens. That was "it" for me...almost...Muffling my laugh, I informed her that I had to exercise the Union County statutes and guidelines and the procedure was that the chickens were to be captured, processed, and then packaged. I then asked how she wanted them packaged; in quarters or halves and asked if she wanted them frozen? By this time, she was almost in tears and so was LB until she busted aloud from the silent 3rd line roaring with laughter. I felt like I was totally going straight to the flames of Hades once again, and would not collect $200!

Years ago LB and I (and several of our fellow consultants) had to meet at the office because our company wanted to film us conducting an estate planning presentation for training purposes. I dislike being on the flipside of a camera. I don't think she was enthused either. Well, after primping for the shoot, my sales manager and I entered the conference room where the cameras were and I was not looking forward to this at all... LB was sitting in a chair primping in a mirror with her back facing us. She swiveled around to us looking so very striking and sharp and smiled at us. She had blackened out one of her front teeth trying to look all Clampett- for the camera. We all fell out with laughter and then LB and I had to go back to the lady's room and clean up our faces. That was beyond hilarious. She is a trip and has been such a blessing and a sisterly friend to me over the years.

THE INVISIBLE ANGEL

Several years ago, I met a very nice lady while waiting to give blood at the American Red Cross. She was not only very striking, but she looked a lot like my beautiful BFF sister, Terry. Although this gal was in a wheelchair, she didn't appear to be bound by it. After watching her struggle a moment to navigate around, she seemingly became a tad frustrated. Acknowledging that the chair was apparently new to her, I eventually and subtly sat down beside her and pleasantly asked if there was anything at all I could do to help her. Within about a 2-hour span, she spoke of the traumatic details about her recent auto accident and the subsequent, painful surgeries. She warmly conversed about her grown children and how she loved and cherished them. We enjoyed each other and laughed and essentially bonded. She had joyously stated several times that I reminded her of her daughter. She said some very nice things that really warmed my heart and made me smile. She asked if I would attend church with her sometime and I said, "Tina I'd love to" as we exchanged phone numbers. We subsequently talked to each other over the phone a couple of times.

One day I left her a phone message. A day or two later there was still no return call so I left her another message. Yet there was still no return call. Had I known her address, I would have gone across town and checked on her. During that time, I received a phone call from her daughter, with whom I had never spoken. Trying to hold back her tears, she weeped as she informed me that her Mom had passed and that she had found my phone number in her mother's home. Yet another point of contact after the death of a loved one. How uncanny is that, I thought. Another petrifying phone call of fatality, with my phone number attached to it. I bet there was a roll of pennies to be found nearby as well.

THE RESILIENT MUFFIN

Sometime later, after traveling to Hartford, CT for 10 long weeks of my aforementioned, wonderful, underwriting training, I became very good friends with a lady from NY. She was married, had a husband and 2 children. They subsequently came to NC to visit one weekend, having family in a neighboring city known as the "furniture capital." When they visited me as well, I made sure to have plenty of food and Kool-Aid for the kids. They brought pickled asparagus and we cooked shrimp wrapped in bacon on the grill. Well, upon this Yankee/Southern visit, I'd bought a 3-pack of muffins (which I rarely eat.) These muffins were the Cadillac of muffins and were a tad costly, not that price mattered, it was the mere principle. Most breads at that time would have nuts or fruit in it. During their visit, those muffins were never touched at all. I thought SOMEBODY'S got to eat those darn muffins, they weren't cheap! So I decided to simply take them to the lake during the next few days to the houseboats where I knew I'd be spending time with Sis and friends over the weekend. I took my guitar and sack of food and those freakin' muffins that I was so anxious to get rid of. Once I got there I simply laid them out for anyone's enjoyment. There were many folks coming and going in and out of the houseboat; snacking and laughing and carrying on. The next morning after I had awakened, my sister made her way outside where her boyfriend and I were enjoying the peacefulness of the calm water and the rising dew as we sipped on coffee. Sis had brought some fruit to the outside boat deck for us and passersby. She's so Martha...but she left behind those muffins! I was certain it was just to get me going about them- again. I went and got those freakin muffins that had become quite comical to all of us. Suddenly, without paying attention to the audience who probably knew what I was getting ready to do, I marched down the hall of the houseboat, opening those muffins abruptly and threw them, one by one into the water. It felt like I threw it 2 miles out and I said a few words, went back and then said a few more words while laughter filled the air. They all truly enjoyed watching me throw my towel in.

Later that evening after a lovely dinner, as Sis and I were washing dishes, we were talking and occasionally peeking out the window above the sink which overlooked the lake, admiring it's beauty. Without hesitation or looking at me, my Sis whispered laughingly, "Hey Vic, come here for a second" as she remained focused on what she was washing. Nodding her head at the window, she said, "look"...As my eyes jolted down to the commotion I noticed that darn resilient muffin bobbing up and down like a buoy, passing right before my eyes as if it was jeering at me. I hope a carp chocked it!

CONOZCO DE LO QUE ESTEAS HABLANDO

My sister Karen and I, accompanied by a dear friend of ours, went to visit the gorgeous city of Charleston, SC, one weekend. Charleston is, as previously mentioned, one of my favorite vacationing spots here in the south.

As excited tourists usually do, we stayed busy shopping and admiring the tasking and talented natives working at the market, watching their creativeness in weaving baskets. We walked through creepy, nearly haunting historical grave sites at night and privately swam in our outdoor hotel pool which had already closed for the evening. One can't much double dare us to do anything. Our dear friend who was with us chickened out on that one. I'll call her Doris as she resembles Doris Day. Doris knew our family very well and had as much fun with us as we did with her. The 3 of us were having a good time while getting spruced up for dinner and a fun night out, and sis and I stretched out on the bed trying to find something quick to watch on TV while waiting for Doris to finish her hair and makeup. As I was flipping through the channels with the remote, Sis shouted "Stop Vic! Turn it back." As I flipped back, what we landed on was a Spanish game show and I quickly remembered that she had taken Spanish in high school. I was always so proud of her for learning the language! Knowing only a few Spanish words myself, I thought, I wish I had made the time to learn Spanish.

Doris was in the bathroom primping and I'm certain tuning in to our conversation as well. As we watched the show, Sis started hysterically laughing at the game show host and guests. Then she would clap immediately as the crowd started clapping and laughing. I thought "WOW, you go girl"! I was so impressed with her understanding of what they were saying and the fact that she remembered the language, especially after many years. Many, many, many, many years I may add.

When I interrupted her several times simply asking what they were talking about, she would flip her hand up telling me to hush. She continued to study the dialogue and follow the show, all while clapping and laughing simultaneously along with the crowd. This went on for quite a few minutes until Doris poured out from the bathroom rolling with laughter, saying, " you know that your sister doesn't understand one freakin' word that's been said on that show don't you"???? Laughing and shaking my head, being the gullible person I truly can be, I turned to Sis and witnessed her crying with laughter, mascara running down her face- and splitting a gut. "You are so not to collect $200 when you go down South" I implied. I rolled in gullible laughter at the scheme. She's always getting my goat. I always told her that she should have been an actress. It's important to learn to laugh at yourself. Life is too short not to let laughter truly be the best medicine.

WATCH YOUR SPEED

As you may well know, my folks had 3 girls. And their best friends of over 50 years had 3 sons. We all grew up together; boating, picnicking, camping, fishing, going to church and of course, went to weddings and funerals. Their family is beautiful and I feel so very blessed to have had 3 gorgeous brothers and another set of beautiful parents also. For many years we've referenced them as Aunt Lucy and Uncle Zeke. They are a very spiritual, intelligent and gracious family whose sons are so very handsome. I used to joke around with Aunt Lucy and tell her I was going to drill a hole in a wall of the house when I went to visit, so that I might "peep" in on one of her handsome sons. Of course I was kidding, however, God doesn't make too many men that handsome.

Well, "Ma-Ma," Aunt Lucy's mother was like my own grandma, and notably one of my biggest fans. She loved hearing my music and compositions and always said she hoped to "see me on the radio" one day. With that said, there came a time in her aging years that my sis and I decided to go and visit Ma-Ma in the nursing home. She was facing a pivotal turn health-wise on entering a higher, much brighter universe; with warmth, love and spirited appreciation. We anticipated our last cherishing moments and memories together with her. Ma-Ma and I sat and talked as sis went out and got burgers and ice cream for us all. During this time, I pushed Ma-Ma slowly around the nursing home in her wheelchair, socially strolling along, trying to stay upbeat and positive and overlook the unfortunate smell of death that sometimes lingers in the air at nursing homes. We were appreciating the present, loving moment, and the precious memories of the past-and smiling about our future- and not being frightened of it. It was a very incredible, spiritual moment that filled the air that day. As we slowly passed by her friends, while wheeling through the warm-spirited halls, she would warmly and respectfully introduce them to me, edifying me as her granddaughter...and as we passed the other wheelchairs I noticed each of the passengers, with huge smiles and extending their hands briefly, exchange high fives as they strolled by each other. They were obviously exchanging and sharing moments that many of us may never notice but clearly meant something exceptional to them. As you may already know, human contact can also be incredible medicine. I immediately felt so spirited, inclined, and emotionally motivated to relocate to their music hall and wanted to tickle the ivory for them for just a bit. All of the beautiful folks began spinning into the piano room and we had some fun, playing and singing as the room flooded with spirited energy. It was so surprising how fast some of them could get around in their wheelchairs! I jokingly began to caution them that I was going to start handing out speeding tickets. They just grinned and chuckled. A little of our time goes a long way to and with folks-especially those who are confined or are less fortunate. Quite demonstrative of how many of us take our everyday simplicity in life for granted. We're all dying every moment of every day, and we are not promised our next minute, hour or day... It was an awesome hug to Heaven, and she will always be truly remembered and missed.

RING-A-LING

I have a dear friend, "Cell" with whom I've had the pleasure of briefly working with in the past. She is so beautifully spirited, smart and funny-truly, and as I grew to know and love her, I realized that she was my common-denominator type of friend. She came by my house after work one day and mentally took me out of my work element, momentarily. As I sat she began laughing at me. Seriously, I thought. "What's up"? I asked her. "What are you laughing at Missy"? What's so freakin' funny I thought? "You just got here"! She said, "I'm laughing already because I know whatever is getting ready to come out of your mouth is going to be a scream"! Laughingly, I replied touche' my friend...touche'." As we sat and relaxed with dimmed music in the background, I suggested that she tell "me" one of "her" funny stories. And of course she did indeed. By this time, mind you, Tracy had arrived and it was once again, the Three Stooges. Now Cell is a plus-sized, extremely witty lady who should seriously perform on stage. Her wit and humor, on top of her loving heart, is so incredible that it will take you to the moon and back. She is beyond hilarious and has a beautiful, gorgeous heart and smile.

Before she started sharing her funny story, she glanced at me, then over at Tracy, then back at me, (pondering whether or not she should be admitting to her forthcoming story) and at that moment I knew this was going to be a good one...and it was.

She began explaining how her cell phone had suddenly gone missing at her apartment and she began getting very upset with her boyfriend, thinking he had hidden it from her: you know how folks get nosy and peruse their mate's phone business. In any event, the more time passed, the hotter she became and started rustling through the cushions on her sofa, adamantly digging into the crevices, but to no avail. She searched her entire apartment making accusations at him and threatening to remove him and his phone from her plan unless he returned her phone. She was so upset and angry with him that she eventually went to bed, warning him that he had better return it by the next morning.

She went to bed angry as all "get out" that night and woke up the next morning hotter than Satan himself. After trying to get a grasp on her day and being in a very angry state, she dove into a warm, refreshing shower, still wondering where her freakin phone was. As she began washing her hair, she suddenly heard a plop onto the floor of the shower. No, it wasn't a curler...her phone had gotten lodged under one of her plus-sized rolls (of flesh that is). Tracy and I (and Cell of course) were crying and laughing, and suggested that she tell no one else about this incident (of where you should never, ever put your cell phone). You wouldn't want to broadcast that story to a writer or anyone who might turn around and alert the media... or Congress.

MAY I SUPERSIZE THESE PLEASE?

Tracy called one day and said "hey Vic- wanna hear a funny"? Again, I thought, seriously? Always my friend, always. What had happened was that Tracy had gone out to a lunch buffet with her roommates one afternoon and was surprised at how much they could " chow down" in one sitting. Now she can do some eating herself but has always been able to stay quite lean. There are names for folks like that I've heard...I'm just saying...Tracy is 5 foot, 10 inches tall. She used to be a model but can truly eat like a horse. A small horse, but a horse, anyway. Tracy had noticed throughout the day that her underwear was unusually uncomfortable and she kept finding herself squirming in a way to privately find comfort. Twisting, tugging and picking at her underwear, she eventually got frustrated enough to do exactly what I would have done; pardon herself from their dining booth and go to the restroom where she gleefully tossed her underwear into the trashcan! She later admitted that when she went to the restroom she realized what she had done that was so annoying and discomforting all day. She had crammed both of her stick legs into one leg hole of her drawers! Bless her heart- and she doesn't even do drugs!

Over the years I've jokingly picked on Tracy and her stick legs, warning her that they would catch on fire if she ran down the street. And being that she has a fairly large head, which even she pokes fun at, I warned her again that she would either topple over first, or catch on fire. These were just friendly words of caution to my dear friend. Years ago, after admiring her thick head of hair, or I should say, envy it- I dared her to do something, knowing good and well that she would do it. She is a lot of fun and is my fellow Gemini soul mate. Watching her for years take "2" long hours to eloquently apply her beautiful makeup (which I learned from my sisters of course, but not the 2-hour part) I dared her to put her hair up into 4 pony tails (one going straight up, one out from each side, and one out from the back of her head. Then she had to go grocery shopping with me, looking so foolish. I knew that I would not be seen with her at all times, but I would be nearby watching. Keeping a good pace behind her, we entered the NICE grocery store and I began crying with laughter as my gut began to hurt. She marched around shopping, neglecting to look at anyone, especially those who were starring at her. I heard someone at the photo counter say "oh, but she's so pretty." Then someone asked me if something was wrong with her (as they witnessed me laughing so hard.) I wanted to tell them that she probably doesn't get out much, although I'm sure they knew differently. She got deep, marveled stares from folks all over that store. It's fun to act a fool sometimes.

KEEPING IT REAL AND SIMPLE

It's important to create internal and external systems that work best for you; i.e., knowing who and what your resources are and how to attain them. Once again, it makes life so much simpler to stay organized by keeping your horse in front of the cart and your head out of the sand. We should understand how successful we can be (personally and/or professionally) by keeping things simply real and keeping them really simple. Know how important it is to work not only very hard, but very smart. Be happy in your pursuits in life- don't ever let any person override or even try to override the power of God and your faith in Him. Always put Him first and keep Him first. Let's not get things too twisted and just simply ease up once in a while. Who wants to be around drama anyway? Stop wasting your time on the rat wheel. Jump off and make sharp, accurate resolutions. Stop wasting your energy and money and keep focused on your tomorrow and not judge and ponder your yesterdays. The obstacles we overcome help make us strong so that we may overcome future obstacles, making our goals more achievable and ultimately our life-long reward. You don't have to have a business title or own a business or be a millionaire to be happy. Just hug yourself in the mirror every day and keep it real and simple. Be proud of who and what you are.

Most of us know that many things are easier said than done. Keep a warm spirit and take long leaps of faith and keep your life and world as structured and organized as possible. Utilize your leadership skills and pave a path for our young entrepreneurs; be a huge, positive and meaningful shadow for someone who can learn from you; and help add a color to the rainbow of our future. Focus on your plate and not that of the Jones'. God never puts too much on us that we can't handle. Sometimes that may sound or feel like an old cliche', but I'm just sayin'...He places precious puppies in the center of our plates and we just somehow have to find it and nurture it- whatever it takes.

Remember "it is what it is" and that we can only do what we can do with what we have at the given time. Be mindful, persistent and consistent. Opportunities knock on our door often that can sometimes make us susceptible to getting tangled up in a web or tumor of confusion, exhaustion, nd sometimes painful disappointments. Keep it real and simple and work one large project at a time staying focused and positive. Walk with purpose and pride and have faith in your capabilities and challenge things to yield rewarding returns. Turn your television off or turn the ringer off on your phone, or simply don't answer it. Leap from the rat wheel you're spinning around and around on like a dog chasing it's tail.   It will exhaust you and may make you dizzy! Remember that if you continue to do the same things in the same manner, you'll continue to get the same results. Remember not to lose your sense of humor and most importantly your sense of self.

THE SOUNDS OF MUSIC

There's a beautiful song I used to play on my trumpet in church called "There's a Sweet, Sweet Spirit in This Place." The song was so beautiful and inspirational and it was all I could do to get through playing it without tearing up. Seeing how much folks were enjoying it was quite rewarding. Many years ago our church had an organist who was blind. Occasionally the church choir director would call me on a Sunday afternoon and ask if I'd play my trumpet at the evening service that night. Again, I do not like playing instruments in front of folks but I would somehow find the strength and just do it. I was clearly on someone else's playing field after all. Being that our organist was blind, I always found it humorous that the church would always have sheet music placed on the piano or organ that he was playing as if he was actually reading the music. You could never tell he was blind and that was so amazing to witness. Not until, at one of the evening services, he slipped and fell into the baptism tank. No, that didn't happen, thank goodness. That would have been awful!

Another Sunday afternoon I received a call and was asked to play my trumpet at the evening church service. Arriving early, I had asked Mr. Henry, the organist, if he'd accompany me in playing the Lord's Prayer (in whatever key that was on my sheet music.) I was so nervous because he was such an awesome musician and I'd never played music with him before. I'd actually never had the honor of rubbing shoulders with him at any length. I was so inspired by him and I didn't want to come across as Granny Clampett- blowing a horn instead of a jug. The first time we rehearsed it was as if we'd been playing the song together for years. I was so pleased and surprised; you could have thrown me on the grill with all of the goose bumps I had afterwards. Once our performance was over, I praised a quick silent thank you, to both him and God. In retrospect, it reminded me of the chilling, energetic and uncanny moment I played "How Great Thou Art" after subsequently writing about my sister, Terry. The moment was incredible and so are the precious memories.

On another Sunday morning, during the sermon, while sitting beside one of my BFFs, Julie, and Rick who is now her husband, I was quickly perusing the church bulletin and noticed it had a huge misspelling in it that choked me up. Per the bulletin, the church ladies were serving "fried children" for lunch rather than "fried chicken." So glad Sis wasn't sitting beside me at that moment. What a ruckus there would have been.

A COOL NIGHT ON THE FARM

Growing up in a city, it was so much fun going to visit the farm. My grandfather was a farmer and all of my cousins lived on or nearby the farmland. They would call me a "city slicker" not really knowing how much country truly flowed through my veins. My BFF cousin, Rob, and I were like brother and sister. I don't know which of us gave the better reuniting hugs each year. He was and still is so much fun. We played multiple musical instruments together and climbed the tallest of pear and apple trees on the farm. He always made sure there were no snakes around me, thank goodness. I hate the word hate-so I despise snakes. We would spend a lot of time together in old tobacco barns plotting our futures and simply having fun in the rural country world. Learning to play the guitar and him playing his drum set and throwing corn to and at the chickens outside the silo was the highlight of the day.

I had to transition myself from being a city slicker to that from where my roots derived. Over a year or so, I had noticed his girlfriend didn't have much to say to me, which I thought was fine. Keep your idle chit chat, and attitude to yourself. It was all good when she found out that Ms. City Slicker was merely his cousin. Ellen, I subsequently thought, had become and has been an awesome friend to me for many years. As a youngster, there was a night when she, Rob and I and some other cousins were running across the grassy lot from his house to my Grandpa's- probably to get some ice-cream or to secretively find a deck of cards (which was taboo to play on a Sunday.) The adults were already nestled away for the evening.

Well, Grandpa had built a humongous chicken coop which was comprised of tons of chicken wire, lots of chickens and a few hateful roosters pounding out their mating calls as if they were playing a piano. The coop was hidden in the darkness of the night and quarter moon. And like I stated, it was quite dark, and we were all running like we hadn't eaten in a week. I had my nice little girly nightgown, overcoat and slippers on and all of a sudden found myself plowing right through and over the chicken coop. I just laid there in Clampett-chicken hockey. They didn't need to use the hose to spray off my dignity this time. I was able to take a shower.

During that time, at that young age, my very meek and quiet Grandpa had sheepishly and very simply asked me to take "the basket" from the back porch and go gather the chicken eggs (as he was enjoying watching the little city slicker doing chores in the country.) But I was determined to prove to him that I could indeed be a farm girl. I knew how to fish and bait my hook, pick beans, shuck corn, blanch veggies, and make homemade biscuits. But, I was too petrified that those chickens and roosters would flock all over me and peck at me like in the Alfred Hitchcock movie "The Birds." So help me if they hurt me I would have them packaged up and frozen! Those roosters looked so mean and vicious and hateful. They truly had evil in their eyes! So I stepped to the back porch and got "the basket" and simply went and gathered all 3 eggs that the 30 of them had laid. It didn't seem like much at all, but I proudly ran across the yard and flew into the kitchen, eager to show Grandpa my big basket of prized eggs. Everyone got so tickled when they noticed that I had taken a laundry basket to the grizzly coop to gather the eggs, but I was so relieved and glad to overcome the fear of the attack of the roosters and to have gotten out of there alive.

"REITERATION"

THE CHALLENGE OF ENDURANCE

Many of us are faced and challenged with multitudes of circumstances and situations. But knowing who your resources are and when to simply raise your hand with pride and dignity when you need something is also important. Years ago, I was working extremely hard at auditioning to be the senior drum major of the high school marching band. This was a thrilling and honorable role to attain and I worked very hard at my choreography and salute for the audition. Right before tryouts, I nearly broke my ankle and I was so very upset over the situation. I had no choice however, but to struggle through the audition, pain and all, and knew that it was important to maintain a poker face throughout the painful process. I simply wrapped my ankle up so Clampett-tight in an ace bandage that I didn't know I even had an ankle. I think of my devoted band director quite often as he taught me so much throughout my journey in music and leadership. I learned to respect and admire him, and became aware of him being observant of my possible leadership abilities even during my previous junior high years when he was also my band director. He had been qualifying band members to play this iconic role basically the same way we have to teach people how to treat us. That was an awesome and entertaining band. It was actually over a long period of time that I truly realized exactly what Mr. Allen had taught me. He taught me that through ambition, strength, endurance, courage, and discipline, that anything is possible. Hats off to him for being so "instrumental" in having faith in me. His $75 is so in the mail.

Don't let people make you feel inadequate or feel insecure about yourself. Just allow God to be the pilot at your wheel (whether it be a steering wheel or the rat wheel) and keep things real and simple. We must learn that we have to keep things simply real to keep them really simple. If your toes get stepped on in life, then perhaps they should have at some point and time.

Sometimes it will hurt for a minute but you'll get over it and you will remember the lesson. Be happy, rejoice every day and be glad in it. Keep your glass half full. I don't care what it's full of, but just keep it half full. Thank God for the beginning of each new day you roll off your pillow. Thank Him for your many blessings and thank Him for the Heavens and the Earth. It's all good.

We all have days that our phone rings off the hook, or we just simply don't feel like chatting at the moment. That's why we have voicemail. Often it's someone trying to sell something anyway, or just a friend or colleague who thinks they are the only one in your world that you attend to. I love my peeps and they know it but it sure is amazing how many acquaintances you have to chisel from your life to recognize and cherish your common denominator keepers. Keep mindful that everyone on this earth needs love but it is indeed important to set and maintain your boundaries. No one can or should live without being loved and it is important that we share love and warmth to others as much as we possibly can. Any couple can make it as long as they both want it but it takes two to tango. It is lonely and empty when there is no love. It is indeed a two-way street. Keep your head held high and appreciate the simple things in life...the chirping crickets and the plump squirrels that eat your grill cover and enjoy learning, the how-to's, and the importance of how to see the trees from the forest. Make animals out of puffy clouds and enjoy life. Don't over-analyze everything and keep things real and simple as they truly are. Share your energies with others and give your neighbor's kid a banana during your busy day and let them bang on your piano for a quick minute. Embrace and cherish your inner peace and nurture it every day. That glow of warmth just may be the "pot of gold" at the end of someone's rainbow.

Try to keep it real and simple with others as well as yourself and always, with God. Embrace and enjoy every day. With time and wisdom, you will eventually learn how to turn your stumbling blocks into stepping stones and focus on where you want to go, not where you've been. Again, add another color to a rainbow and let your inner peace smile with warmth and spirit to others. Thank God for His many blessings and don't forget He has a sense of humor too. Understand that we all make mistakes and that God is a forgiving God- continue to ask for His forgiveness and always keep it all good with Him. Keep it real and keep it simple, knowing that it's all good, through God. Remember what his Son did for us and never forget those footprints and His bleeding feet and heart. Relish with spiritual comfort as it will carry you through its' boatloads of highways and crossroads.

Refrain from finding fault in others and tend to your own plate. Take care of your mirror, not the Jones'. Stay focused with your individual program and keep your head out of the sand. If you teach people how to treat you, life may be more complacent- just like coasting down a hill on a bicycle riding with your arms in the air cheering, "Look Ma- NO HANDS"! Be mindful that others have a story too and they may need you to open your heart to listen and hear them. Each and every one of us is a unique fingerprint just as the meat of a nut confined by its shell. Keep mindful that it's your pillow that you must sleep on every night and it's your mirror you have to face every day and remember to hug yourself daily. Keep it real. Remember that the bad day you may be having is only for a moment- and that the sun is always out; we just can't always see it. Stay positive and focused, keeping your horse in front of the cart by keeping things in perspective. Veer from constant procrastination and tackle the bull by the horns. Wash your sink full of dishes that seems to be overflowing-knock it out and set yourself up for enjoyment of the next meal. Make positive and joyful things happen. Remember that God created the Heavens and the Earth and we should walk in peace, happiness, harmony, and unity. Don't overload your plate and be alert and mindful of your surroundings wherever you are and remember one important thing: wherever you go, there you are. It's as simple as that: one, two, three. Pick yourself up and dust off your bottom when you fall and stop being a whiny crybaby. Whahhh! As Flo says, "sprinkles are for winners."

Try not to take things for granted and appreciate the conveniences in life. Hug and value your neighbors and friends; thank and praise God every day when you arise to your new given day. Maintain peace, tranquility and the freedom you deserve in your life and steer clear from obstacles that may interfere while doing so. When you are going through a difficult time and simply need a guiding hand, remember the footprints in the sand by which God has embraced and comforted you. Understand that you are NEVER alone. Have the utmost appreciation of what others have done for you and for simply being who they are. Wrap them a Christmas present of love that lasts forever because we are never promised tomorrow. There is nothing like "this present" and nothing like giving "a present" to a loved one especially when they desire "presence" rather than "presents."

Refrain from merely entertaining ideas and goals. Take further steps and make things happen. Make your goals and ambitions happen via affirmation because they are all achievable even if you don't have a large cheerleading squad with fancy pompoms. When you put your heart, passion and energy into something you truly believe in, you'll find how strong you really are, especially if you allow God to be your ultimate cheerleader.

As an analogy, consider your goals like climbing a mountain. When looking up you may perhaps feel intimidated by the challenge and reality of this enormous rock of life. Refrain from staring at it for too long- contemplating, analyzing, procrastinating...You already knew you were going to climb it before you spent $75 in gas to get there. As your adrenaline starts to flow, you hoist that rope UP to the top of the mountain finding excitement in the journey for which you had already planned and properly equipped yourself to make. You may experience a few falling rocks but you knew it was a mountain before you started climbing it and you cautioned yourself of the possible obstacles of those falling rocks. You had ample opportunity to digest a closer view while you were glaring at from hundreds of feet behind where you just left. Embrace that feeling and know that every ounce of sweat is indicative of the joy of accomplishment you had set in your mind to attain and the triumph of success you will feel.

Once you get to the top of that mountain and take a deep breath, you can do a 360-degree pivot at that moment, smile, and see that everything and everyone is beautiful in God's own way for once, and perhaps in yours too. There were 3 steps here; initially where you "were," your starting point- comfortable and positioned and grounded as your adrenaline began to race; secondly, the "journey" which was your action for your goal, or simply "the climb"; and then simply...your "achievement"- when you conquered that seemingly invincible mountain after drinking your Red Bull. It was as simple as you made it, because you kept it real and had faith in yourself. We can't always selfishly expect immediate results as patience is always a virtue, (a virtue that carries a lot of WAIT.) Keep your life and dreams as real as possible and GOD will make the impossible happen. You'll experience multitudes of happiness and accomplishments just as the strenuous climb of the mountain you just conquered.   You just have to do it.

WALTZING WITH KARMA

I've noticed that folks get things very twisted sometimes. Makes me wonder if they've ever had a ripe green rose switch popped to their pompous ass before. I'm just saying...many of us should stop being so selfish, so ungracious, and so unappreciative by taking things for granted with an "I CAN'T HAVE NOTHIN' attitude. We should all be very thankful for the things that we have and not dwell or complain about the things we don't have or what we feel we've been deprived of.

Seriously, whiny hiney? Let's focus on reality and the present and resort to the common denominators of not only our friendships, but also our perceptions, perspective and values of life itself; remembering the concept that yesterday you were 5, and when you awoke this morning, you were 90. We only turn 29 once in life, however, some of us a little more often than others. Once again, never forget-wherever you go, there you are. Let's stop looking down our nose at others in judgment and again, tend to our own plate. Realize that when you point your finger at someone else, there are always those three fingers pointing straight back at you. We are all so extremely guilty of being judgmental; whether we walk into someone's house and observe; or witness someone being out of sorts; or view anyone else in a perspective other than your own ways. If you do any of these then you're being downright judgmental. We can call it what we may but it's being judgmental. Again, it's not all about you. Karma will make that pointing finger of judgment bruise your head. Period. Just because someone does something a certain way, or doesn't do things the way you do things, or simply looks a certain way, or sees things differently, doesn't mean that it's incorrect. Just because someone sees things differently than you, simply means they see it differently. It's a matter of perception and that is why we sometimes "agree to disagree."

My older sisters and I never had children (nor did we ever eat fried children)! My parents didn't judge us for that at all. They are probably glad that there aren't anymore like us! I'm just stating an overall opinion. It seems to be so much easier for some folks to stoop down to someone else's level instead of rising up (or manning up) to a higher level themselves. We will all ultimately be faced with one judge some day and I hate to say it, but with all due respect, it ain't gonna be you. Believe it or not. It won't be the Clampetts either. Just sayin....

THE GEM IN I

While dealing with individuals and couples regarding their business or personal issues, I've truly learned the importance of how to keep things as real and as simple as possible. Sometimes I have acted in the capacity of being their consultant and/or sometimes their friend. Either way I've recognized mounds of accomplishments in not only my world but in so many others that I have been blessed with having as my prized common denominator friends. I tip my hat and applaud them all for their passion, strength, integrity and their uniqueness. Previously I have stated that by simply being a Gemini- I love my little motto- there's a "gem in I and there's a gem in you too." Sometimes however, it does get a little unnerving when folks call to get my advice on the same issues over and over and over again and it's frustrating to witness them going around and around on their rat wheel. I understand that there are many ways to skin a cat per-se, but you will more than likely get the same answer from me on the same issue on the 3rd attempt as you did on the 1st attempt, unless the facts or issue itself has somewhat changed. Once again, if you continue to do the same things in the same manner, you will continue to get the same results. It's as simple as that. Although helping others is a passion among many of us, it can however, be somewhat challenging. We all are living busy lives, yet I find it so gratifying and spiritually and emotionally rewarding to just simply make time for others through the grace of God. Almighty God has given me the strength and ability to testify and share my wisdom during my journey of life. Don't get upset with advice when things don't work out on your behalf because you merely didn't try anything different to better the situation. At that point and time, you will definitely get my bill for $75 for the Clampett-ass headache you've given me and/ or others. Change can be good. It's all good.

Utilize your resources and keep your boundaries in check, and periodically reassess your values and your overall purpose with margin and reason, concentrating on body and soul. Take your own simple advice and courageously go out on a limb on occasion with the understanding that your first instinct is usually correct (that's the "gut feeling" you sometimes have.) Be strengthened and encouraged through the fundamentals you have learned while growing up. Exercise your talents and sharpen your skills, and share your talents and spirited gifts with others. Give a huge hug to our strong veterans and let them know we appreciate them and their service, and open that heavy door for that sweet little ole' lady (who could probably use a hug as well.) Volunteer and donate some of your precious time when you can to help out others such as the elderly at nursing homes or at your local food banks or establishments for the underprivileged. We never know when our good friend, Karma, will be stopping by for a surprise visit now do we? Be prideful as you look into the mirror when you rise from your comfortable, fluffy pillow to yet another beautiful day that God has blessed you with and give yourself a hug if you feel worthy of it. Each day that we wake up to is a precious gift. We should live each day as if it was our last one, taking in and giving back all that we can. Pray the simple prayer for God to simply "lead, guide and direct you to happiness and success." Success doesn't necessarily mean a realm of wealth of money in my mind's eye, but rather it means the wealth of spirited peace and harmonic happiness and a sense of achievement and gratification. Be open-minded to take God's cues, taking direction and finding and understanding your uniqueness and purpose. His advice is without doubt, priceless. Not to mention that it's free. I haven't gotten a bill for $75 in the mail from Him yet. Once again, stay alert and be open-minded for His cues. Be careful what you wish because it just may come true.

Although I care about people very much, He has more time and energy than we do for each other here on earth. Simply "do unto others as you would want done unto you." Always, not just sometimes- let's not make that optional- so that others around us can find comfort, peace and happiness in your spirited company.

RESPECT

There are two simple requirements that most of us ask of others, subconsciously in many instances, and that is for mere respect and privacy. When you learn to simply teach people how to treat you and reciprocate the same courtesy you will typically earn the same from them in return. That type of ease in attitude and contentment may keep us all in check, grounded, and on the same page with each other.

If you tell someone that you are going to do something that involves them, respectfully follow through with it responsibly and reasonably (unless one foot is in the ground) as to not waste anyone's time. That's an all-time pet peeve of nearly everyone. No one likes that sort of nonsense impeded upon them as an individual, nor should we be selfish and inconsiderate and waste someone else's time- at least give them a fair heads up if that's the case. Let's get with the program because it ain't all about you and your time clock. Most everyone has an agenda and/or schedule. It's the same concept as how we often train our pets about obedience and the wrongs from the rights, by diligently executing the sharp verbal command "that is NO"! Also, speaking of having one foot in the ground and as a simple reminder, please make sure that your personal will and powers of attorney are prepared before you truly do have issues at large and perhaps one foot in the grave. Procrastinating in taking care of these types of matters can lead to very hairy, scary, and not to mention nasty issues with the family and with the state. These issue can become a little iffy in some cases. Just simply have your secretary call their secretary (figuratively speaking) and take care of your responsibilities by making things happen. Whether you're here on earth, or pushing up daisies, no one likes the burden of taking care of your broken pieces, especially when there were things you could have done about it. Take the initiative to make things happen before the issues become so large that they cannot be mended. Leaving a family behind is difficult but leaving a broken family behind is even more difficult. I'm just sayin...

PRIVACY

The pleasure and privacy of our homes is something that many of us enjoy and expect and is included in our mortgage. Yet it has become quite comical. Sometimes you can just sit back watching other folks rubbernecking-either through their mini-blinds or just passing by on the street simply trying to keep up with the Jones'. We're all people watchers to a certain degree, but some folks are just downright nosey! I'm not being judgmental here, just factual. Period. There's a big difference between rubbernecking (like folks do when they're passing a car with a flat tire on the side of a very busy interstate) while everyone else sits in heated traffic for over a Clampett-hour, with screaming kids, blaring radios, irate in-laws, the "I gotta pee syndrome" and the "I'm thirsty" and "are we there yet" repetitions, all while searching for the UNICORN that doesn't exist, and looking out for your neighbor. I've been so blessed with having some of the most fantastic neighbors a community could ever ask for. They are beautiful, spirited, and kind-hearted folks with such disciplined and respectful children and fun-loving pets.

When folks noticeably caught wind that I, Ms. Vicki, had been working on having some things published, so many people would approach me with their same spirited desire. I just simply said to them that If I can do it, anybody can. Make things happen. Like anything else, it takes a lot of determination and even more dedication and discipline- a half full glass of each. Not to beat a dead horse, but we truly do have to keep it simply real before we can make it really simple, and many things are only as hard as we make them. Everyone is a unique story. Everyone is a defined fingerprint and every person has their own unique story. I admire and applaud ambitious people who follow through with attaining their goals.

Not long ago, as I briefly mentioned before, I was faced with having to personally install new doorknobs with dead-bolts in the office door of my home in order to safeguard some of my private documents from one of my tenants, who in particular I had noticed trying to enter my office with a skeleton key made from paperclips.

The bottom line was that he'd wanted me to have his music (that he had previously written) published without him having to put forth the effort in doing so. Ms. Clampett doesn't work that way. We already had an agreement that he would reside, rent free, in my house (as merely a tenant and colleague) in exchange for his work in my estate planning business. Instead, he was apparently marveled by my genuine nature, accommodating offerings, and southern cooking. It didn't take me long to adamantly advise him that I was not barefoot, I was not pregnant, and I was most definitely not his pseudo-wife (which wouldn't have been bad had I been interested). I was also not his servant. I work hard for my money, so go make yours. That's why I enjoy my peeps for knowing and respecting me for who I am and for whom and what I won't be. And I have the utmost appreciation for the common denominator friends and friendships I've acquired. We need to understand each others beliefs, expectations and how we systematically roll- and to simply have respect. This concept has worked for me for many years- 29 of them, over and not quite over again.

MAGGIE

It's amazing how people really come through for you when you least expect it and perhaps at a time when you need them the most, especially when you don't know that you need them until they smile at you and say, "Look, you've had my back- let me have yours a minute..." Invaluable and precious. Priceless. Spirited and so greatly appreciated.

Not long ago my awesome friend Maggie stopped by my house for a quick visit as I hadn't seen her in quite a while. We chatted on the patio before she came in and as she glanced around and got comfortable in the den she basically noticed the stacks of work I had everywhere, neatly organized. She could see that I was quite exhausted of multi- tasking, wearing many hats including being a landlady, working on my writing momentarily, and working with my estate planning duties while trying to find someone to help me with it. She could also see how I've power-housed trying to maintain my old money-pit of a house, now that all of the free-loading tenants have been booted out. That's a legal hurdle of a chore in itself. As a landlord, I don't think it would be too complicated to make living arrangements a tad difficult to disrespectful tenants. It gets cold in the winter here in the Carolina's, especially for folks who aren't going through hot flashes. I'm just saying...You wanna stay; you've got to pay, or go away. OK?

Seeing how I'd been wearing many hats and had become mentally and physically exhausted and depleted of fun time, Maggie looked at me and said , "Vic-I've seriously never seen anyone work so hard. You've had a lot on your plate and need to take a break." That's when she spontaneously began packing a few pieces of my clothes into a duffle bag and said that I was going with her to the lake for a couple of days.

I initially resisted but eventually when Maggie became adamant, I threw my hands in the air and agreed. She took me to a large, sunny, beautiful fun-filled lake for the weekend, joining several of her wonderful friends. They had large, gorgeous boats (a Clampett-jon boat would have sufficed) and as I was taking in all of the relaxation and fellowship, the guys suavely pulled the boat upon a sandy embankment of a small island so that we could splash around awhile.

As Maggie stepped off the front of the boat she bent over and quickly picked up a penny-shining in the sun and and tossed it at me, laughing and stating, "Terry's here and wants us all to have fun"! And indeed we all did and it was all good. It was awesome, taking me out of my stressful element and knowing that I had not had fun in quite some time. That type of medicine is beyond what any doctor could order. I met so many wonderful people out boating that weekend and it was a reminder of how important it is to take a fun-filled break from busy, worldly things and how I'd missed being in that type of joyful environment. Just simply getting away from drama, the exhausting work and the unwelcome drama of being a landlady, was incredible. The feeling of warmth and spirit in the company of beautiful people and crisp glistening water at the lake was more than refreshing for the body and soul.

PENNIES, PENNIES, AND MORE PENNIES FROM HEAVEN

Not long after that lovely weekend, I made a quick stop by the local strip mall near my home to make a few purchases-and "no stripping"- was involved. I swung by my local branch to pay my phone bill and as I entered, I noticed something glimmering by my loafers (no, not slack people, but my shoes.) Ironically, as I looked down I was surprised to see a stack of pennies and I don't mean two or three of them-or even a roll of them. I simply mean they were stacked up tightly. I didn't notice anyone nearby playing jacks, dueling banjos or strip poker for that matter, thank goodness. All I could figure is that if this was Terry's way of contributing to pay for our means of communication, then I'd need to start finding a lot more pennies than what was in the stack I had just found. Actually, I should be sending her a check for $75 in the mail for showing me that history speaks for itself. Her prominent words of wisdom and loving, prideful encouragement have been so comforting and will linger forever, regardless of what mysterious side of the coin I pocket.

SHARING THE CONCEPT

When you are organizing yourself, your life, your work or whatever you endeavor to do to "scrape your plate off" remember to keep things real and simple and that through God, it truly will be "All Good." If and when you start noticing that this concept works for you, let others in and show them how simple it can be to lead a happy, fulfilled life. Thank God Almighty every day for His many merciful blessings and hug yourself in the mirror as you stand nose to nose with yourself. Don't get trapped in a web of other people's attempts to make you feel lesser than them or their expectations and realize that it's merely their angled, judgmental nose that needs to be chiseled down a notch or five.

In going to DC to attend the aforementioned, exciting seminar, I simply learned to exercise my keen decision-making abilities and utmost energies, recognize my cues and accept guidance from not only God but from my newly met acquaintances ("cheerleaders") from FL and Canada. I also learned to be open-minded and spontaneous as necessary. It was "my choice" to accept guidance from my own personal cheerleaders here on earth in addition to God's guidance, and my choice to be trusting, positive, and open-minded about this motivating venture to DC (after completing my "homework" in order to rule out any skepticism on my part.) Stay true to yourself and the CONCEPT itself will indeed set you free.

MM (MOTHER MARY)

I have a very special red-headed friend who many of us call MM (Mother Mary.) She is like a mother to me and has a billion of so-called "children" including myself. Yet another common-denominator friend whom I've had the pleasure of knowing for many, many years. She's just a little longer in the tooth than me, and somewhat wiser. I spent an awesome week with her sometime ago in FL., along with one of her "other children." She is an insurance agent like I was "back in the day" and is spunky, hilarious and smart as a whip. She surely isn't a Clampett-whip. She doesn't "mess with the dumb stuff," previously implied by Terry. She doesn't tolerate nonsense at all, and I love it. Her birthday is one of the few I can remember because it's the 29th of October and we've both been 29 and holding for quite a while.

I recently sent her a birthday card that was very funny. It was vivid in color, having about 8 red, yellow and blue finches perching on a clothes line. One of the finches was hanging upside down and in a caption bubble that read "Happy $^#@ Birthday." It opened up to read , "Pardon my Finch." It was such a jovial greeting card to have cost only 50 cents at the dollar store. "Priceless" as MM would say. It's amazing how inexpensive things are at the dollar store, but you really have to know how to be frugal, and not fooled. Knowing what's a good deal and what's a totally Clampett-deal is important to recognize, just as much as knowing that it doesn't have to be big or expensive to put a smile on someone's face or make them laugh.

RENEE

MM is an incredible friend, just as hardworking as her daughter who lived with me briefly some years ago. Thank goodness her daughter had been living with me because one day a fire broke out in the towel closet in the hallway of my house and she was inside the house when it happened. I was outside doing yard work. Due to our opposite schedules, we seldom were at the house at the same time. In this case, she and one of her friends flew out into the backyard where I was working, screaming about the smoke that suddenly began engulfing the house. Quickly noticing where the smoke was coming from, and not opening the door of the culprit, we expeditiously grabbed the fire extinguisher, a water hose and called the fire department- all at the same time. We were indeed a multi-tasking trio. The fire department arrived shortly after and thank goodness, pass the gravy, it was all good. The fire had resulted from a defective wire in the doorbell unit which I had subsequently disengaged, of course. After a whirlwind of handsome firemen rolled out of the candy apple fire truck, they were ultimately very calming, and proud of us to have handled the situation so quickly and sensibly. I would love to say that we all went on a wonderful cruise the next week to get over the trauma, but we didn't. We were all, however, so very glad that not much damage took place and that we were able to still see each other. Literally. SOMEONE was looking out for us on that beautiful day. Thank you for all of the pennies Terry!!!

Another friend of mine has passed unfortunately, but now lives in the loving comfort of Sis and many others. I mention her in remembrance of how genuinely special she was to many of us and really made us smile and laugh. Years ago, and in another city, when friends would gather at my house, Renee would stop over as well and watch (and sometimes help) with my yard work. Giving constructive criticism, she used to laugh at me for "burying" my shrubs in lieu of "planting" them. I didn't think I planted them too deeply. Perhaps she was viewing from the wrong angle.

Remember, I said earlier that it wasn't right or wrong, just a matter of perception. Little did I know it would soon be from the right "angel." In retrospect, she was the one who applauded me and my "green thumb" for keeping the prettiest, healthiest-looking fern in the neighborhood. I had it hanging in my den for a few years, always looking so full and pretty. Little did she (or anyone else) know that I'd been going to Walmart every couple of months and replacing the fern with a healthier one! Shush, don't tell.

KNOCK, KNOCK, WHO'S THERE?

When you simply crack open a nut, it's tough at first to get through the hard shell, but once it's opened, you realize that "our shell" is merely a fraction of who and what we are, internally and quite simply, externally. In my mind's eye, we are large components and elements of something or someone, and to me, that someone is Christ. When I found myself through Him, again many moons ago, it gave me the realization that our shell is only a sheer fraction of who we are...who we will always be... and where we will always be. When you find yourself through God, never, ever fear death. As stated in one of my old songs I wrote long ago entitled "Don't Question God," I wrote " for He's prepared a home for us and it's a glorious place.." With God's continued guidance I will have my songs published one day. Until then, just remember to keep it real, keep it simple, and I'll keep writing. It's all good, through God. Embrace Him always. More times than none, it's not the actual fear of dying that petrifies some of us, it's merely the fear of not living.

JUST DO IT

In my journey of life, I suppose I've learned to engage in having a "just do it" attitude so that I refrain from wasting too much time and energy over-analyzing and pondering things. Sometimes I think we just need to simply get things off of our plate because life is too short. Way too short. I often think about the fact that yesterday I was 5 and when I woke up this morning I was 90. Analyzing obstacles and affiliated hurdles can be so very challenging and strenuous- many of which are simply downright Clampett-in the depths of our own perception, and yet some of which we really didn't "sign up for." But it is what it is. Many of us have a tendency of being over dramatic about things and forget how important it is to keep things simply real and to keep them really simple. My attitude, with regards to my quick decision to attend the seminar in DC, was that I did not have time nor want to make the time to orchestrate this spontaneous, and somewhat financially, burdening venture. At the time, I was dealing with two different estate planning entities, practically getting nowhere, and had a Clampett-non-paying tenant, and a yard, and a...SERIOUSLY? Calgon, take me away already! We can add all of the "ifs, ands or buts" in our passionate desires, "but" I felt the importance of leaping into my cue of being more instrumental in life and perhaps growing from it in the process. I contemplated the trip over and over, Ms. Clampett-drama mama here, until my dear friend "FL" made the wonderful mistake of sheepishly advising me to "practice what your preach, Vic." I remember hesitating and chuckling in a snarling way saying "bite me- see ya there." Without knowing the hows or whens, I set my mind to it and again it was quite a meaningful, worthwhile trip after eliminating all of the ifs, ands, and buts from the ultimate equation.

Take your issues at hand and keep them as simple as possible. Walk a positive walk and talk a positive talk, and strive to be selfless and understanding of others- being mindful that not all "plates" are molded to accommodate everyone else's life. Simply focus and tend to your own personal plate and the deck of cards you've been dealt. Treat yourself as well as you do others. "Listen" to others as well as yourself and strive to enhance your skills, your world and your life. Find that adorable, fluffy puppy on your plate and simply love and nurture it. And safeguard them both, in all tender significance. Keep perspective in order to keep up in this fast-paced world we live in. Write a heartfelt song or meaningful poem sometime- or better yet- merrily waltz to the beating drum of them both.

THE STURDY HATRACK

After many months of wearing numerous hats, I found myself getting more and more exhausted- physically and mentally. Being a homeowner, a landlady, an estate planning consultant, and my own domestic engineer, I had reached the realization that it was beyond time to perhaps end the stressful burdens that homeownership had saddled me with for so long and to simply "practice" what I had been preaching- to get off the ongoing rat wheel, let God take over the steering wheel, and make a big-girl decision. Shewwww, what a cumbersome mouthful of struggle I felt! I once again asked Him to lead, guide and direct me into happiness and success. I had always made these massive decisions professionally, so why not make a personal leap (of faith)? All I wanted was a little simplicity, less hassle and drama-and I knew that it wouldn't come knocking at my door. Ed McMahon never did, so why would "Simplicity"?

For a long minute it seemed like such a drastic decision to be making without seeking guidance or advice from anyone-perhaps feeling a bit alone in my own little pity party (whahhh and boo-hoo) but it was my decision to do this privately, on my own, and to perhaps avoid unwanted or unnecessary opinions of others. Less is more most of the time and, once again, I indeed triy to "practice what I preach" (figuratively speaking.) I remained mindful that I had the utmost guidance and strength from The Almighty.

The physical part of owning this money-pit of a home entailed not only maintaining a large yard filled with trees (raking and bagging roughly 40 gallon bags of leaves each Fall and removing large, heavy and bulky amounts of tree debris), but the fact remained that I'd been twenty-nine and holding for several years...(not quite a dinosaur yet.) Considering all of the factors I had on my plate, I didn't hesitate to keep the horse in front of my cart and make a positive, healthy change in my walk of life. I was beyond anxious for a change to less stress and a happier/more relaxed heart and sense of well-being. Strategy, with a hint of endurance and persistence- encased with ambition and a desire for more colorful, brilliant rays in my future were well in order.

After carefully evaluating the direction of my so-called horse and cart, and anticipating the pleasantries of a little more freedom and comfort in my future, I made arrangements to sell my house and move on. And so I did.

DO MY OWN HAIR AND MAKEUP, THANK YOU!

I contracted with a friend in real estate and in a matter of time my home was sold. I rounded up a posse of friends to help me with this colossal move and found it evermore exhausting than what I had anticipated due to my lack of experience, I'm sure. I never realized how much tangible nonsense (and intangible for that matter) one could keep over a dinosaur duration, not to mention how many Clampett-items we truly hoard! It is quite shameful, but I was very happy to donate some sentimental items to a local church which included my old piano, lots of office furnishings, and other whatnots that could be replaced. I had already removed my tenants and their drama to complete avail. I knew it once again was "All Good" and I was looking forward to riding a new wave, life preserver, surfboard and all...

My plans to live with my dear friend Cell were in place. She was currently out of town due to a death in the family. Until then I was comfortably lodged in a hotel, privately rejuvenating from an exhausting move. I invited my moving crew over to the hotel for a quaint celebratory dinner in recognition of their hard work and to help indulge in the victory I felt in moving forward from such an overloaded part of "being." Although I had paid them quite handsomely, you can never pay a friend or anyone else for that matter, for the respect and regard they give you during a transition to a happier life. We had all shared cartwheels during this strenuous move it felt. But I knew I had joyfully clipped the strings from residing in the long-aged mammoth of a neighborhood; having a true compassionate realm of family-oriented neighbors was precious, but having a stressful strand of proven impossibilities was not what I had ever signed up for.

During my stay at the hotel, I had texted Cell a quick note asking her to let me know if there was anything I could do to help out with her aunt's funeral. The funeral was local and I knew that some of her family was going to be staying with her momentarily. I offered to cook and/or clean her house; just simply do what we gals do when it comes to family and/or funerals.

The next day as I was out and about, she called me and in her peppy, fashionable voice, implied that there was indeed something I could do to help out with the funeral. My immediate thought was that she would take me up on my offer to cook or shop, or tidy up her house, but on the contrary! She indicated so meekly on the phone that her request was for me to "do" the hair and makeup of her deceased aunt. Shock was what I felt, instant, real shock. A few seconds passed after which I heard a roll of laughter. Thank goodness because I am definitely not a licensed cosmetologist by any means, nor do I want to be! I do my own hair and makeup, thank you and that's it!

I AM WOMAN, PASS THE GRAVY

Soon after this brief delay with my living arrangements, I contacted a friend and his wife who had owned rental homes here in Charlotte. I just knew that he would "have my back" as I did his when he didn't have a room for one of his tenants I had previously housed. Fortunately, he did have a room at this time, so we made arrangements for me to rent a vacant room in one of his rental homes, graciously being remanded from the expense of my unexpected hotel stay and curve ball of an avenue I had to take.

Within a few days I had settled in and become acquainted with my surroundings and fellow tenants. I was able to feel relaxed and content-especially with the physical and strenuous move I'd recently made. One should be ashamed of hoarding so many furnishings- TV's, fax machines, phones, and whatnots over such a long period of time...) "Out with the old and in with the new"! I held on to only those things that couldn't be replaced... Terry's trophies, pool tournament jackets, family photos and anything else that was sentimental and sensible to keep.

It was a mere three nights of being settled in my new humble yet temporary abode, while sleeping comfortably in my bed, that I heard a jarring of the bedroom window, located behind my head. Being awoken so abruptly at about 2 o'clock in the morning, out of what I hoped was perhaps a dream of being disoriented; the opening of the window became intense as did the heavy stampede of feet landing on my head. Two masked intruders were aggressively breaking through my bedroom window, using my head as a welcome mat to enter the house. Shame on them for frightening me and waking me out of my precious REM sleep! I was beyond floored and scared absolutely to death, but no pun intended. I was neither a floor mat nor a Welcoming Committee for this invasive intrusion. This is not what I'd signed up for...at all. After getting a brief glance at both of their awful-looking face-masks, I promptly covered my face beneath my warm blanket and prayed a quick subtle prayer..."If it's my time to go, and you want me now dear Lord, then I'm ready...but please don't let me suffer..." In other words, let them shoot me in the head and get it over with, I don't want to get beaten, stabbed and/or raped. Boy was I thinking hard and fast! After feeling the ice-cold barrel of a cold pistol steadily held to my temple and the intruder's nose to my ear, asking who was under the covers, I replied in such a feminine voice "just me." As if he knew who "me" was. I just wanted him to know that I was alone and was not a threat; and that I was a woman. Won't roar quite yet.

After they recognized that I was indeed alone in my bed, and me still feeling the cold barrel of his soul at my life, he calmly assured me that if I remained quiet, I would not get hurt. Not a problem I thought- I'll sign up with that plan; however, I was in complete shock and trembling with fear and disbelief. I'd never experienced such a fright in my life! Never.

As I heard the two of them leave my room to enter the other parts of the house, I heard my roommates in the background anxiously communicating on the phone with the police. Soon after, the glorifying blare of police sirens became the highly-welcomed sound of praise and saving grace! Hallelujah and pass the gravy! The entire boat of gravy!! We're having a gravy party! We were incredibly shaken-our minds frozen in disbelief as crime scene investigators and canine units engulfed the house in a matter of minutes...dusting for fingerprints and searching for any other evidence of who these robbers were while consoling our shaken demeanor. We kept it real, as simple as possible, knowing that it would all be good, through the grace of God. And it was. Not only because we were not harmed, but the blessed uniforms soon captured and convicted the thieves. I hope their wardens scare them awake each morning...come on back and step on my head one more time, Mr. (I thought)! I'll make Cujo help you polish up your slobbery manners. It didn't take a rocket scientist to realize that I didn't need to continue residing at this location and Cell, in return, expedited her efforts in accommodating my moving in with her. She and I had been great friends for years and had been sales associates together at a couple of previous marketing jobs. We had always "had each others back." She always had mine, and I always had hers. She and her family have always been like a family to me, and I welcomed the forth-coming time of living with her and enjoying humorous times, which we did. She was extremely supportive with the big-girl decisions I had recently made and the determination that I had in jumping off the stressful rat wheel I had been treading. By simply "practicing what I preach" while continuously connecting my dots, I was approaching a more joyful and deserving place in life.

WELL, TUMBLING TUMBLEWEEDS!!!

I comfortably resided with Cell during the next few wintry months. While there, Cell shared with me that a friend of hers had a nearby staffing agency and was offering some part-time work. It would be a great supplement to getting back into the business industry I'd been accustomed to. After a brief phone consultation with the rep at the agency, it was indicated that I would be doing some "marketing work" for a very large golf company that was liquidating their business assets at one of their locations. Although I had detected a gigantic red flag during this chat (I would need to "dress warmly") I consigned myself to the task. I chuckled when I arrived at the golf store the next day, knowing that I was not going to be a senior marketing rep, but would more than likely, be doing something stupid and Clampett- and, freezing my tail off doing it. And I was right.

Suffice it so say, I promptly found myself standing out in the freezing cold at a major NASCAR Motor Speedway intersection holding a 9-foot tall Clampett-advertising sign while holding onto a stop sign during the brutally windy cold bursts of what felt like Alaskan Arctic air. I don't know who laughed harder- the folks who passed by laughing at me, or me laughing at what a fool I must have looked like to them. There was no shame in my game as I was completely wrapped in warmth from head to toe and no one would be able to identify Ms. Clampett herself. I had laughed at the green Liberty Tax folks before and always wondered if there was a little ounce of fun in it for a few days...and there was...and I made it the last one.

Several of us had re-positioned our "advertising" posts and my new standing point was located at an intersection in front of a steak house. A very nice, aromatic steak house, I might add. That particular cold and brutally, windy day, one of my cardboard signs suddenly and briskly blew off of my 9-foot Clampett-wooden pole. Unfortunately this was shortly after I had just been briefed by a co-worker that tornadic wind gusts were forthcoming. Ya think? I had to literally swing from tree to tree to capture and repair the sign and slid into the restaurant for a cup of hot coffee afterwards.

I could tell the workers there found this to be quite entertaining because they were laughing "with" me as I walked in and gave me coffee on the house. I was being applauded for the endurance and stamina I had sustained. Certain I'm sure, that I could swallow any undignified feelings down with a strong hot brew... I gave it one more shot until the next tornadic gust not only totally demolished all three parts of my sign which I quickly released, but had blown me to the ground, tumbling as I grasped onto the bending trees! How ridiculous, I thought. I felt like a Texas tumbleweed! I finally threw my so-called towel up into the air and went back into the friendly steakhouse and shared a few more laughs with the kind folks. Ironically, it was called The Texas Tumbleweed Steakhouse and they therefore proclaimed me to be their official tumbleweed mascot.

THE ASSAULT

After having made substantial long-term living arrangements with my dear friend and colleague, and after several memorable months of residing with her, Cell approached me with the surprising news that she was going to relocate back to the Deep South- to the big city of "Hotlanta." In turn, and with great excitement for her, yet to my personal dismay, I knew that I had to make yet another temporary move until a more permanent living arrangement could be made for me. Exercising patience and due diligence was of great essence at the moment as I knew that keeping my glass half full and not empty would be quite challenging; but I knew "it would all be good."

Soon after I tendered a preliminary week's stay at a quaint hotel nearby until my new move became more deliberate. During my brief hotel stay, I met a seemingly nice couple who had checked into the same hotel just prior to my arrival. They were residing just a few rooms down from me on the same floor. Friendly, sincere, and family-oriented they seemed; showing me pictures of their children-and an array of their prized family photos. They demonstrated a sincere respect towards me; a feeling of honesty and trust in just a mere two shadows of a room away from me, sharing a few nice brunches with each other in the main lobby.

Then early one evening I heard a tender knock at my door and heard her asking if she could borrow something. Not hesitating to let her friendly voice enter my room, and in an effort to accommodate her request, I kindly rose from my peaceful rest to let her in. Unfortunately, she did not hesitate to disengage me and my friendly hospitality. She forcefully plowed her way into my room while her hidden counterpart followed, thrusting me back onto my bed.

It was as if a tremendous lightning bolt was abruptly striking me while I was forcefully being secured behind closed doors. They thrashed me back onto my bed demanding me to be quiet. I squealed like a frightened cat in hopes that some friendlier neighbors would hear my SOS. Their tight clasp around my screams and neck, along with their steamy glares was indicative that they meant business. A silent business. They tried so venomously to muffle my crying shouts which were nothing that I was accustomed to by any means. It was at this brutal moment when I realized that I was a victim in an extremely violent scenario. What had I done to them to deserve this torture? I wondered.... Nothing at all, I thought while realizing these folks were apparently some sort of devil's advocates- folks I'd never previously met, thank goodness. I totally could not believe what was happening, nor did I understand it. I'd been somewhat of a renowned professional in the Queen City for many years and have never tolerated any type of nonsense...but this was directly in my face at the moment and I had to cope in the most mindful way that I could. My personal strength, faith and endurance by which I live was unknown and uncared for by them. Meanwhile thinking, once again, "didn't this kind of crap happen to other folks"? What a selfish thought I admit-but it was what it was and all I could do was try to survive through this massive and painful situation and become callous throughout their brutality and many hours of horrific beatings.

They both gradually (and simultaneously over an approximate 15-hour period) beat my head and face trying to halt my cries of pain; thrashing me onto my bed. Then they propped me up to my feet and sucker-punched me a few more brutal times in an attempt to seemingly knock me into silence- while they resumed their efforts in robbing me of my personal belongings; obviously I knew by now that I had completely been scammed since day one. They hastily removed my hotel phone from the wall while confiscating my cell phone for obvious reasons. In between further excruciating beatings, I simply tried to ask them what they wanted. Whatever they wanted, they could have if I had it. But apparently they wanted to have a little fun in their seemingly warped world, and I wasn't in the mood for their violent version of fun. As I felt my face swell, my private prayers escalated.

Along with each blow to my face and head, they began to remove the earrings from my ears and my cherished school class ring from my hand. Realizing they were obviously after money, they apparently didn't realize who they were dealing with: Ms. Clampett-herself. I was not the moneybag they apparently thought I was, but I was emotionally stronger than they imagined.

After I had screamed for them to simply take my wallet and/or debit cards, they seemed to have found I was getting too loud; so they proceeded to forcefully squash a pillow over my face to hush me up, nearly choking me into silence. I got quiet alright, but that wasn't enough for them. So they proceeded to knock me back down onto the hotel floor once again, this time by grasping heaping fistfuls of hair on the crown of my head, dragging me by that clasp into the bathroom. I learned quickly when not to whimper as they had no problem hitting me a few times during this horrid journey. While lying on the bathroom floor like a limp flounder, they plunged my head into the toilet bow, over and over again, viciously banging each side of my face and head over and over prior to dunking my head into the toilet bowl. In retrospect, it was undoubtedly a slam-dunk situation and was getting absolutely more and more frightening. I unfortunately have a slight hearing impairment as a result of this, but it's all good.

I had already given them the pin number to my debit card and after hours of the attack, they finally decided to listen to some sense from me. Plain ole' common sense. And while exercising my affirmations and personal prayers, I immediately began to feel their worth, the prayers, that is. These thugs were of no worth to me at all. Using my attempt to use reverse psychology, it didn't seem to take long for them to realize that they were digging a deeper and deeper hole for themselves. And at that particular moment, I truly did not know how I was alive. But then again, yes I did. The purpose I already believed I had...

They finally became somewhat tired and took a moment to breathe and plotted out their journey to go use my ATM card. She was to stand guard over me in the hotel room so it appeared, as he went to retrieve the minimal Clampett-funds from my bank account. I had honestly given him my correct PIN. She then watched and actually became human for a few moments in his absence as she anxiously awaited his return.

He was furious upon his arrival because he didn't get cash from my card. I knew at that time that he apparently didn't use it correctly as I'd undoubtedly had given him the correct PIN. Thus the brutality started over. I was completely exhausted and limp, but was glad I'd eaten some protein that day. I was once again beaten and drug to the bathroom for the repeated slams of the porcelain throne and dunked yet over and over into it. My cries for mercy became louder and louder. I was subsequently drug back to the bed to lay as they attempted to muffle my cries with "the pillow." I then heard them conversing about running a bathtub of water...to drown out my cries and to ultimately drown me. Kill me! And then I heard the water running...running and running to the extent that I felt the subtle steam. Talking about having to think fast and harder...I did feel it was considerate of them to run a little warm water into my deathbed. Stick a fork in me at this time, I thought, because I was

141

done and done-er. Well done.

I'd never been so scared in my entire life suffice it to say. I knew that my parents had already lost one daughter, and I could not bear the thoughts of them losing another one, especially in yet another tragic and violent fashion. So I quickly came up with a plan of my own. I was beyond and over being a play toy in their idiotic way and world. The underlying fact was that he was using the card incorrectly. I thought that if he didn't know how to simply use an ATM card, then he had a few more personal issues than I thought. I wasn't being judgmental; I was simply being observant. What were these folks after, I wondered: Clampett-money that I didn't have? I had some, but not much. The two of them proceeded once again to indulge me with their beatings and viciously drag me across the floor by the crown of my thin hair, smashing my head back and forth onto and into the porcelain throne. It's ironic how we all have different interpretations of the meaning of "throne."

Somehow, I boldly talked him into going back to the ATM once again while I politely convinced him that I was indeed giving him the correct PIN. As the joyful brightness of the morning arose, I began to feel the warmth of the sun. And Son. "Game on suckers" I thought, you're on another battlefield as of now!

I then quickly decided to play possum in his absence and "fall asleep." I lay so very lifeless on my bed of torture, knowing and fully aware that this was my true chance to get the heck out of there. In this case, I thought, you both really can collect $200, but I'm the one who's fixin' to "get outta jail." "I'm ready to get outta here, I thought"! My dad used to say that while boating over intrepid waves. His words of wisdom had once more stuck with me in all graciousness.

While I laid there with one eye half-open, and with him still being out there on his mission to gather his not-so-Clampett-funds of mine (literally speaking this time) she quickly arose from her bed and walked very quietly to the bathroom. I thought to myself, you can jump into that hot of water and kiss my fat white cellulite tail, cause I'm out of here sister! Bite me! And furthermore, shame on you two!

Like a tethered rubber band, I nervously darted out of the hotel room and nervously jolted down two flights of steps when I heard Ms. Theatrical venomously yell down at me through the echoing wells. I didn't know what she was foolishly screaming but quite frankly my dear, I didn't give a you-know-what. I just kept dashing. Not knowing how marred I must have looked; I walked into the main lobby and kindly asked the attendant to call the cops. Not giving a "care" to my appearance, he replied that I had to make that call myself. "it was procedure." I thought, "are you freakin serious"??

I firmly clasped my hands around the sides of the counter and grimly told him to his eyeballs that procedure needed to quickly change unless his attorney was sitting in the back office, and I meant it.

After he made the call, the police arrived in a matter of minutes. They were completely disgusted with this robbery and with my brutal beating. They proceeded to take multiple pictures of my face. They were so absolutely upset and adamantly proceeded to do their legwork. To my surprise, I wasn't in that much pain, probably due to shock or maybe because of the mere excitement of being alive. They immediately started viewing hotel videos while one of them went upstairs to find the room empty with a bathtub full of cold water. Thank goodness for videos, uniforms, and Karma. I was eventually taken to the hospital to be examined. Having been in shock from this unsettling attack, I had not had a visual of myself at this point and time and was much alarmed when several of the doctors were looking at me like I was a freak...a look that said "I'm surprised you're alive"! I then took a hesitant and alarming look into the mirror, and I truly didn't feel like hugging myself at that moment. Not physically. I didn't even look like me. I'd never been a fan of Frankenstein, but I looked like the bride of one!

When I finally found myself able to calmly reflect, I was blown away by this horrific attack. I was positively and overwhelmingly grateful to be alive. All I knew was that I was scheduled to be at work that same day, within several hours. I knew my new job would make an exception for me to "call out" which they so graciously did. After the medical staff ran a few tests, a nurse entered my room and advised me that someone was there to visit me. OK, I thought- get their full name, date of birth, place of employment, mother's maiden name, shoe size, social...take a snapshot and fingerprint them and bring it to me...not their head, but simply their name. Then and only then would I agree to see anyone after what I had just gone through. Seriously, it truly frightened me. I asked her to find out who the visitor was because I had only called two people regarding this; my supervisor, and my friend who was a tenant of mine. The nurse soon returned, advising me that my visitor was Sal, (my co-worker/mentor at my new place of employment.) She had quickly caught wind as to what had happened to me and I was so moved to see a familiar face. There had been no time for me to do my typical hair and makeup and I knew she would freak out from my new look. I had not allowed anyone other than doctors to come to my room, so I went to greet my friend in the waiting area.

Holding my head down at first, I gently glared up to witness the blood rush from her head to her toes, white as a ghost. She gave me a warm and sincere bear hug and I quietly whispered and assured her that I looked a heck of a lot worse than I felt. It was all good. She was in disbelief but within minutes she became my pal, "Sal."

Soon after, Sal sent a sincere text to our work stating that I was indeed OK, and still witty as always. Several days later, I returned to work and could not have asked for a more gracious, sincere and heart-felt return. I could have returned sooner than I did, but when my own personal banker didn't physically recognize me right after this attack, I could only imagine what my retail customers would think about my horrid look behind hoot-owl glasses and a part-time orange, yet soiled, apron. I had to physically present myself and speak with my banker for them to recognize who I was.

It was the sunny Month of May, and the flowers in my lawn and garden department where I was employed seemed more vibrant and smelled more brilliant than ever. I once again felt the irony of being surrounded by one of the only things I'd missed about my money-pit of a home of over 20 years. People didn't seem to annoy me as much as they used to. It was so much easier to let things go and not whine over spilled milk. I began to have a greater appreciation of each and every one and each and every thing. Inasmuch as I've already written and spoken of virtue, and expressed the importance of listening, loving and appreciating, and to exercise patience, I felt it all beginning to surface; the importance of keeping positive and maintaining your glass half full.

START SPREADING THE NEWS

Let others know how much you care about them because we are definitely not promised tomorrow; nor the next day, hour, or minute. Praise the day and praise God that you exist, and have the opportunity of truly living that day, and living in it. I have been so thankful and joyful to be waking up on this side of the ground since that horrid incident and frankly before then as well. Gratefully, I practiced what I had been preaching for all of these years by personally reiterating to myself that I have a purpose here on this earth, and no one, and I mean NO ONE will take that from me. When it's my time, it's my time, and I'm ready. Until then, I will continue to hug myself in the mirror; comfortably sleep on my pillow at night; be thankful of the running water and of the green grass on this warm side of the grave that I awake to every day. I am so thankful to relish in the joy of the chilled glass I have been provided to keep more than half-full of positivity; thankful and blessed of everyone and everything- especially that I was never raped or murdered, or shot or stabbed; that I have all of my limbs and senses; my family and friends; and that I am able to witness the growth of the perishing plants and their vibrant blossoms that I see and smell as I enter my work daily while they, (my plants) patiently wait for a new home where they will be able to put a smile on someone else's face, just as they do mine. But, as I am entering my work or wherever I may walk, I am most thankful for simply "being."

Please understand that Christmas is not all about lights and presents; it's about the brilliant light of the absolute present, "LOVE." Perhaps slow your life down a notch from the microwave world we have evolved into and reach for your dreams and wishes wholeheartedly.

There is indeed a reason for each of our lives. Each and every day should be a celebration of life and what your worth is to that day and to yourself. Make every day a reason for any season. Enjoy each and every day of life, even when you can't see the sun; remember that the sun/Son is always out and that sometimes we just simply can't always see it. "Remember to remember" as I was once told... Connect your dots and understand that there is indeed a purpose for you and your life and embrace each day with spirit and appreciation. We are all God's creation and He deserves the best from us in return. Keep things in perspective with valued appreciation and not in frail wonderment. "Out with the old, and in with the new," whether it's something tangible that you feel needs discarding, or a friend who is not seemingly one of your common-denominator's...or even a mere habit. Just keep it real, and keep it simple. Change is always good when you can connect your dots and realize your purpose; or that you simply have one, or perhaps you are one. The least we can do is to be the best we can be and find what our purpose is. It might be to just be a better person in general, a better friend, neighbor, aunt or cousin; sister, co-worker, employee, husband, or wife. Just be the best you can be because no one can hide behind or from God's radar. Remember that you will not walk this earth forever. Know that through God's grace and mercy He has an eternal, gracious and blessed place for His precious children. Keep it real and keep it simple with the complete understanding that He will always provide for us. Keep connecting your dots with diligence and dignity and simply find your purpose. I think that perhaps I have finally found mine. And maybe, if I'm remotely accurate, you just read it. To God be the glory.

I had to simply practice what I had been preaching for many years, which was to evaluate all things considered and hop off of the rat wheel I had apparently been on. I simply had to embrace my own personal prayer for God's wisdom to continue leading and guiding me in the direction of success and happiness in which He has historically lead me.

Keep it real, keep it simple, IT'S ALL GOOD, THROUGH GOD.

II Timothy 4: "I have fought the good fight, I have finished the race, I have kept the Faith."

THE END

Made in the USA
Columbia, SC
14 February 2019